ANCIENT CITY HAUNTINGS
MORE GHOSTS OF ST. AUGUSTINE

ANCIENT CITY

MORE GHOSTS OF ST. AUGUSTINE

Dave Lapham

Illustrated by
Tom Lapham

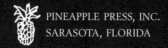

PINEAPPLE PRESS, INC.
SARASOTA, FLORIDA

HAUNTINGS

To Sue as always, to Joanne, and once again to
St. Augustine, the Ancient City

Inquiries should be addressed to:

Pineapple Press, Inc.
P.O. Box 3889
Sarasota, Florida 34230

www.pineapplepress.com

Library of Congress Cataloging-in-Publication Data

Lapham, Dave, 1939-
  Ancient city hauntings : more ghosts of St. Augustine / Dave Lapham.— 1st ed.
        p. cm.
  Includes index.
  ISBN 1-56164-307-6 (pbk. : alk. paper)
  1. Haunted places—Florida—Saint Augustine. 2. Ghosts—Florida—Saint Augustine.   I. Title.

  BF1472.U6L37 2004
  133.1'09759'18—dc22

                                                    2004003818

Printed in the United States of America

ACKNOWLEDGMENTS

A very special thanks to Bill Cook, Charles Tingley, Carol Bradshaw, and Reis Libby of the St. Augustine Historical Society for the tremendous assistance they provided, not only with historical data on the Oldest House, but also with the historical information on the rest of the Ancient City.

A special thanks also to Neil and Betty Morgan, who put me up on many cold winter nights, and to Jennifer Pastore and Kristine Howe for their help and encouragement.

And thank you, too, to all of my tremendous friends in St. Augustine for their stories and their encouragement. Happy haunting to you all.

Once again I relied heavily on *The Oldest City*, edited by Jean Parker Waterbury, St. Augustine Historical Society, St. Augustine, Florida, 1983; *The Gonzalez-Alvarez Oldest House*, by Jean Parker Waterbury, St. Augustine Historical Society, St. Augustine, Florida, 2000; *Mary Evans, A Woman of Substance*, by Patricia Griffin, St. Augustine Historical Society, St. Augustine, Florida, 1977; and other historical records of the St. Augustine Historical Society.

CONTENTS

Preface
9

Introduction
10

The Old Jail Museum
12

Antique Mall
24

The Painted Lady
32

Ghost Tour
44

Herbal Creations
50

Castle Warden
56

Casa de la Paz
66

The Oldest Wooden Schoolhouse
72

The Spanish Washer Woman
78

Casa de Sueños
84

Scarlet O'Hara's
90

The Minorcans
96

Dogs and Demons
106

Crumpet of Old City House
110

The Pumpkin Church
116

O. C. White's
122

The Kenwood Inn
132

The Oldest House
140

Ghost Magnets
146

Old St. Augustine Village
154

Sanksville Cemetery
160

The Warriors of Moultrie Creek
167

Ghosts of the Matanzas
174

Sightings
178

In Closing
189

PREFACE

*T*he number of ghosts and the amount of paranormal activity in St. Augustine continues to astound people. Ten or twelve years ago, St. Augustinians did not talk about spirits, perhaps the only subject they didn't address. Now, there are about a dozen different ghost tours. Ghosts have become big business in the Ancient City, and with good reason. Everyone loves a good ghost story, and ghosts abound in St. Augustine.

As I did in *Ghosts of St. Augustine*, I have again altered names and places in some of the stories to protect the privacy of individuals, and I would ask those readers who like to track down the locations of the stories to be respectful and sensitive to the people involved.

I hope you find *Ancient City Hauntings* as interesting and enjoyable as you found *Ghosts*.

INTRODUCTION

*A*fter publishing *Ghosts of St. Augustine*, I had intended to begin work immediately on another book of ghost stories. I was much intrigued by the ghosts in that wonderful, historic city, and I had developed a passion for them, even though I hadn't yet seen one. But then the book came out and I was overwhelmed with book signings, talks, and other endeavors. And, I must admit, I was a bit taken with the small celebrity I was receiving. So the days and weeks stretched into months, and, after my initial rush to collect new stories, my head began to turn to other pursuits. I lost interest in ghosts.

But they hadn't lost interest in me. Every time I went to a book signing, whether in St. Augustine or elsewhere, people had stories to tell and always asked me when I was coming out with another book. I would answer that I was working on it. But my heart wasn't in it.

Then one day, my friend Jennifer, who had accompanied me on my first ghost tour, called. She had some things she wanted to show me and invited me over. She was insistent. And she did have a lot to talk about, so over breakfast one Saturday morning she asked me where the house in the "Gateway to Hell" story in *Ghosts of St. Augustine* was located.

"Where do you think it is, Jennifer?"

"It's on the Island, isn't it?"

"Why, yes. Do you think you know which one?"

After breakfast, we got in my truck and went across the Bridge of Lions to the island. She directed me down A1A. "Turn left here. Two blocks down. That house on the right. Is that it?"

I was dumbfounded. "How did you know that?"

She proceeded to tell me about her theory of the Matanzas massacre, a story that I will relate later.

After I dropped Jennifer off, I went up to visit a friend, an antique dealer on San Marco Avenue. We talked for a while and then decided to stroll down the street and go into a few more stores. In each store we entered the subject of ghosts always seemed to come up, and each person we met had a tale to tell. Were the spirits trying to tell me something? I took the day's events as a resounding "yes!"

In one afternoon my passion for the ghosts of St. Augustine was rekindled, and I renewed my desire to have a face-to-face encounter with one of the spirits of the Ancient City.

Crazy Alice is a tour guide at the Old Jail Museum on San Marco, a short distance north of the Visitors' Center. The Old Jail has some interesting history, and Crazy Alice makes it even more interesting. She doesn't exactly scare you, but she does challenge your comfort level with the gruesome details of prison life. Alice plays the role of a female prisoner, and visitors are new inmates she's showing around. Of course, it's all in fun, but when the tour is over, you find you've learned a lot about jails in the later 1800s and early 1900s and about this jail in particular.

In the 1880s St. Augustine was a thriving, growing city. Henry Flagler had come to town and the place was jumping. His Ponce de Leon Hotel, which is now Flagler College, was filled with wealthy tourists from the Northeast. Unfortunately, the old town jail sat nearby on Cordova Street in plain view of everyone, and it was a real eyesore. Henry was not a man to let something like that go unnoticed, so he offered the County Commissioners $10,000 to build a new jail—away from his hotel, a long way away.

The County Commissioners selected a site in North City, several blocks north of the City Gates, paid Mr. J. W. Estes $2,500 for the land, and hired the Pauley Company of St. Louis to build the jail for the princely sum of $17,912.35. One might note that Pauley also built Alcatraz and several other high-security prisons around the country. This jail was high-tech for its time. It boasted a four-feet-thick concrete ground floor, two-feet-thick concrete walls and ceilings, a newly patented, revolutionary locking system, and twenty stout, high-security cells, which would accommodate seventy-two prisoners. Of course, there was no glass in any of the barred windows, no light except what shone through the windows, and no heat, no water, no sewage. The structure consisted of two wings with a breezeway between. The north wing contained the jail, the south wing the residence for the sheriff and his family. The sheriff's house was not quite so austere as the jail.

The outside didn't look quite so bleak. The structure was one of the city's finest examples of Queen Anne–style architecture with Victorian brickwork. In fact, visitors newly arrived in St. Augustine more than once went to the jail thinking it was a hotel. The neighbors were quite happy with having the jail nearby, because it was such a lovely building.

And besides, they had a good sheriff who kept the inmates in order. Charles Joseph Perry was sheriff when the new jail opened in 1891, and he remained in charge until 1919, except for four years at the turn of the century. Sheriff Perry was a big man, six-foot-six and three hundred pounds. And he was hard. Prisoners were criminals and they were in jail to be punished for their crimes. He kept a pack of dogs out back, just in case any inmate was foolish enough to try to escape.

Conditions were harsh in the jail. For the men there were three floors of cellblocks all built in the center of building. These cells might have been cold in the winter, but they were comparatively dry. The women didn't have it so lucky. Their cellblock of two cells was on the ground floor on the east side of the building next to the outer wall, which meant that they got rained on and were visited by all sorts of snakes, bugs, and other critters. Fortunately, women who committed crimes were usually either incarcerated in a sanatorium or put under house arrest in their own homes.

Bedding consisted of a straw and Spanish moss–filled mattress, a wonderful breeding ground for red bugs. Each prisoner rated a blanket, but blankets were rare. And, of course, the only clothes a prisoner had were those he or she was wearing. Since there was no water, except drinking water, which was strictly controlled by the guards, no one ever took a bath. The only sanitation available was a bucket for each cell, one bucket for four prisoners. Sick prisoners were kept with the general population, and there were more than a few deaths from disease, especially dysentery.

Although there was occasional meat, the prisoners usually ate grits for breakfast, were given cornbread or hardtack to take with them for the noonday meal if they were going out on a chain gang, and returned to beans for supper. There were no fat prisoners.

Rules in the jail were arbitrary and changed often, depending on the whims of the sheriff and the guards. Infractions were severely dealt with. The most common punishment was solitary confinement for a few hours or many days.

In 1877 a convict lease system was instituted whereby businesses could rent prisoners to work in a variety of capacities. It was a boon to businesses because the rent was low—and went to the jail, not the prisoners—and there were few controls on the treatment of the convicts. They worked long hours in cotton fields, turpentine processing plants, lumberyards, and railroads. There were often no provisions for food or shelter and no protection from the excesses of overzealous guards. But governments at various levels loved the program because it brought money into their coffers. Businesses loved it too, because the labor was so cheap. The general populace hated it. Escapees knew that if they could break free and reach a country home the occupants would help them. That's where the term "home free" came from. The system was eventually abolished in 1923.

Capital punishment, of course, was fairly common. The usual method was hanging, and the jail had a gallows in the back next to the big live oak tree. Whenever there was a hanging, all prisoners were marched outside to watch. Sim Jackson had been convicted of murdering his wife and was sentenced to hang. He approached the gallows scaffold carrying a bouquet of flowers and singing a hymn. With heavy feet, he walked up the stairs where he reluctantly gave his bouquet to Sheriff Perry while the hangman put the noose around his neck. He refused the whiskey offered him to steady his nerves, and before the hangman placed the black hood over his head he spoke to the crowd, "Farewell, my friends, goodbye, meet me in Heaven, I am going there."

The hangman secured the hood on his head, checked the rope to make sure it was properly set, and pulled the lever. The trap door sprung open and Sim Jackson shot toward the ground. Jackson had agreed to cooperate with a medical experiment to determine how long the executed remained conscious and if he felt any pain. He did not struggle after the drop, but through a prearranged series of hand signals he did signal to the two doctors standing beside his dangling body that he was in pain. He responded only to two questions. Fourteen minutes after the trap door had sprung, Sim Jackson was declared dead, and the local undertaker, R. A. Ponce, carted off his body. That was the last official hanging in the jail, which remained in operation until 1953.

As one can imagine, the Old Jail is haunted—very haunted. In fact, it is in the National Directory of Haunted Places as well as on the National Registry of Historic Places. Dozens of paranormal research teams, psychics, mediums, sensitives, and even NBC have gone through the place. None have ever left disappointed. When Historic Tours of America, Inc., bought the property, they added an evening "Ghosts and Gravestones" tour because of all the sightings, sounds, and experiences people had at the Old Jail.

Ed Swift, director of operations, spent two months with the previous owner, Melvin Bair, to learn as much as he could about the place. Mr. Bair complained about the sickeningly sweet odor they couldn't seem to get rid of, like the sweet smell of molasses. They were constantly having the maintenance people cleaning, trying to rid the place of the odor. Finally, Mr. Bair asked Jennifer Pastore, one of my local sensitive friends, to come in to see what she thought about the smell. She toured the place and just shook her head, "You'll never get rid of it. It's the sweet smell of despair." Psychics explain that in death there is often pain involved, especially with hangings, and there is almost always a sweet smell that pervades the area at the time of death. That odor often lingers or comes and goes.

Mediums Carri and Will Donnan, who own The Painted Lady B&B down the street, also came to provide their impressions. As Carri approached the jail she heard dogs barking and found out later about the sheriff's dogs he used for hunting down escapees. She also heard people talking, shouting, and moaning, smelled food, and sensed a lot of female energy in the kitchen. She distinctly heard male voices singing "Swing Low Sweet Chariot" and "Good Night, Irene." She also heard chains being dragged around. Months later, a paranormal research team recorded the same sounds. While

Carri was still outside she sensed a man sitting in a rocking chair whittling on the porch. Several weeks later, while doing some landscaping in the front, maintenance workers found a whittler's rusted knife buried in the ground.

On her first visit, Carri sensed a prisoner named Charley, who ran away from her when he realized she was aware of his presence. After repeated attempts on subsequent visits to communicate with him, he finally let her know why he was afraid. As Carri related the story, "He told me he was raised Southern Baptist and all his childhood was told that if he were bad he would spend eternity in Hell. Well, now, he was no angel, and he had been a criminal of sorts but nothing bad. But he was sent to jail and sentenced to hang for a murder he did not commit. He thought his brother or brother-in-law had framed him. He was actually hanged for the crime, and his soul remained in this dimension, because he was afraid that if he moved on, he would go to Hell. I felt so sorry for him."

And at the edge of the kitchen Will discovered a short, stocky, muscular man, maybe a Greek, but obviously of Mediterranean descent. He was wearing a pullover open shirt with stripes and regular long pants. Around 1910, apparently, the jail changed to a pullover, striped shirt uniform. The man looked quite hot, and he was just hanging around the kitchen, perhaps another lost soul for Carri to rescue. Months later Jennifer Pastore, who had previously helped Mr. Bair, also identified a male presence pacing the hall between the women's cellblock and the kitchen.

Crazy Alice's tour is entertaining, educational, and fun, but the nighttime "Ghosts and Gravestones" tour can be downright scary. Late one cold winter's night, I met John Stavely, Historic Tours of America's national director of historic entertainment, and several members of his team for an after-hours tour of the Old Jail. I parked my truck and walked toward the entrance. The gate was ajar, but I saw no one around. I was still twenty yards from the building and already getting the willies. Maybe this wasn't such a good idea, I thought, and where is everyone?

Just then John came out the front door. I breathed a sigh of relief. He saw the look on my face and laughed. The "Ghosts and Gravestones" tour guides are really into it. They enjoy the subject matter, but after a time they all become reluctant to go alone into the building. And it's a gradual thing. In the beginning, they don't mind. They know the history. They understand what this building was, and it's not a big deal. But then so many things happen to them. They see things, hear things, get touched or pushed. It's pretty scary at times.

"I've been on three psychic walks through the place, paranormal research investigations, and the interesting thing is that all these sensitive people always report hearing and feeling and seeing the same kinds of things in about the same places every time, in the same spots. One woman started upstairs, stopped, and went back down. She said that was not a place she wanted to go. And in the women's cell on the left we're told there is a sort of malevolent force. People get pushed and tripped and feel sad there. Those are the areas we try to be careful in."

One of the guides, Sean, said that he sometimes hears scratching on the walls up in the cellblocks. Another guide saw a crouched figure in one of the cells as she was leading her group on a tour. The figure looked at her and darted off right through a wall.

Sean had been working there for about a month when another guide warned him to be careful because some of the guests had been complaining about a smell in the building. Sean just thought his coworker was teasing him, because he was new. But when he opened the front door and entered, he was overcome with the foulest smell of human feces. He quickly closed the door and gathered himself, his tour guests behind him. When he tried to enter a second time, the smell overpowered him, and he ran off to nearby bushes, doubled over with nausea. Melissa, Sean's friend who was also there, said that on the previous tour an hour earlier, there was no trace of the smell. "It just filled the whole building, but the next morning, the odor had completely disappeared."

John pointed out that "this seems to be one of the signature episodes of the place, and there's no explanation for it. Except for the short time in the early 1900s when there were showers upstairs in the cellblock, there has never been any indoor plumbing or sewage system. We've torn the place apart, and we've never been able to locate the source. It comes and goes in cycles. We'll have periods when it will occur for a day or night or even linger for several days. Then we won't be bothered for a long time."

Sean remembered something. "The morning after that happened with the smell, our safety officer, Ken, came in about 7:30 in the morning to get something out of the safe we keep our stuff in. He was the first person here that morning and the only person in the building. He was opening the safe and he heard something. He thought someone was coming in and he said hello. No one answered. He shrugged and started opening the safe again, when he heard this 'evil laughter' behind him. The hair on the back of his neck stood up and his spine tingled. He jumped up and raced out of the building. When he caught his breath, he went over to the depot area where the drivers were just beginning to gather and asked if anyone had been over in the jail. They all looked at him kind of funny and said they'd just got there and were finishing off their coffee. It really freaked him out. He doesn't like to go in there by himself now either, even in the daytime."

John added, "You never feel like you're by yourself inside this building. Maybe some of that is my imagination, but there are particular spots where the hair goes up on the back of my neck and my skin just crawls. I feel as though someone's lurking somewhere just staring at me."

"It's just like he says," Melissa joined in. "There's always this eerie sensation that there are other people here with you. One of the drivers came in here, in the parlor of the sheriff's house on Halloween, looking for the Book of the Dead—that's the basis of the whole tour, trying to find that—because it wasn't where it was supposed to be. So he went in to see if anyone had moved it. He walked into the room and to the left of the fireplace looking around for it, and as he was coming back he looked in the far corner, the southeast corner of the parlor, and he said there was a luminous figure sitting in one of the chairs. It frightened him out of his wits."

John responded, "The interesting thing about the building is that it's not common to see apparitions. It's more common to see shadows, movement out of the corner of your eye, to hear things, footsteps, voices, whispers, moaning, chains dragging. So, it's fairly uncommon to actually see things, but it does happen, as Melissa pointed out. We have a maintenance man, Vince, who is pretty sensitive, and he has also seen people. Once he was outside on the south side of the building and a lady in Victorian dress walked by. He didn't think anything about it because there's always someone around in costume. He just said hi and went back to his work, but when she didn't return his greeting, he turned to look at her—and she was gone. Another time he saw a stranger outside and approached him to ask if he needed help. The man just walked through a wall and disappeared. Vince even went over to feel the wall to see if something had changed he didn't know about."

Another guide, Justin, said he was standing up in the cells one night talking to a group of people and felt someone pushing him in the back. He looked around and saw no one, so he just figured he was imagining things. But then he felt a hand run slowly down his back. He said he had tears in his eyes he was so scared.

And Andrew, another guide, went in to turn off the light that shines on the chair upstairs. Before he ever got to the rheostat, which is near the dumbwaiter, the light slowly faded, and he was standing in total darkness. Like most others, he raced out of the building almost in terror.

My after-hours tour of the Old Jail Museum was over, and John led us all downstairs and out the front door. I was glad to be outside. We said our goodbyes in the parking lot and I climbed into my truck. As I was driving out into the street I felt a tremendous sense of relief, because I had truly been frightened. Crazy Alice would have been pleased.

from any Barnes & Noble store. Without an original receipt, a store credit will be issued at the lowest selling price. With a receipt, returns of new and unread books and unopened music from bn.com can be made for store credit. A gift receipt or exchange receipt serves as proof of purchase only.

Valid photo ID required for all returns, exchanges and to receive and redeem store credit. With a receipt, a full refund in the original form of payment will be issued for new and unread books and unopened music within 30 days from any Barnes & Noble store. Without an original receipt, a store credit will be issued at the lowest selling price. With a receipt, returns of new and unread books and unopened music from bn.com can be made for store credit. A gift receipt or exchange receipt serves as proof of purchase only.

photo ID required for all returns, exchanges and to receive and redee
dit. With a receipt, a full refund in the original form of payment w
and unread books and unopened music within 30 d

TOTAL PAYMENT   10.00
CHANGE   1.05

Thank you for Shopping at

B. Dalton Booksellers

#269522 07-28-05 12:57P BHA

*F*or much of its existence St. Augustine ended at the Old Gates. There were Indian settlements, of course, and a few who farmed there, but for the first couple of hundred years not much happened in the area of what is now the north end of San Marcos.

After the United States gained possession of Florida in 1821, Americans began streaming in. Ft. Mose was established as the first free black community in the United States. And toward the end of the nineteenth century Henry Flagler began his now famous (or infamous depending on your point of view) development of St. Augustine. The Abbott Tract was opened just north of the Castillo and houses were quickly built for the managers who worked for Flagler on his railroad and various other enterprises. Development sped north.

Today the north end of San Marcos is a collection of homes and stores, many of them dealing in antiques and collectibles. In fact, that section of San Marco just north of Ripley's is now called "Antique Row" or "Antique Alley." You can tell which buildings were originally built as homes—they're set back off the street for privacy. The stores were built right on the street for easy access. The Antique Mall was built in 1901 as a neighborhood store, which carried tobacco, confections, dry goods, and sundries, something akin to our own local convenience stores today.

James Clemens was a successful Savannah businessman who had a wayward, philandering son. He had spoiled the boy and continued to enable him as he grew into adulthood. He tried everything to settle the young man down. He saddled him with as much responsibility as he thought his son could handle without ruining his business, but his efforts were useless.

Finally, James Jr. met a nice young woman and fell in love. His father was ecstatic when they married. He wasn't happy for long. Young James soon went back to his philandering ways and became an even bigger embarrassment to his father.

Exasperated, the senior Clemens looked around for some place to put his son where he would be out of the way, somewhere where he couldn't get into too much trouble. He decided on the backwater town of St. Augustine and built the store where James Jr. and his pretty young wife lived on the second floor.

History does not record whether he mended his ways, but we do know that he died alone in his bed in the middle room upstairs. I prefer to believe that he saw the error of his ways and had become a good husband.

After Mr. Clemens' death the building changed hands several times but continued as a store of one kind or another. Susan and her husband, David, had been antique dealers in St. Augustine when they bought the place a few years ago. They decided to establish the building as a mall, where individual antique dealers rented stalls.

Both the downstairs and upstairs were rented out.

When they bought the place Susan wanted to give it a new look—remove the worn red carpet and repaint throughout. One evening she, David, and several others were working late, moving things around, and tearing up the old carpet. David was working downstairs pulling up carpet when several books on a bookshelf fifteen feet away came flying across the room and landed at his feet. The bookshelf was standing by itself. No one was near it. The books just catapulted off the shelf to the other side of the room, landing at David's feet. Susan and David were a bit unnerved by this, but the previous owners had forewarned them, so they accepted it. Mr. Clemens was not happy with all the noise.

A few nights later he was really upset. Michael, one of the dealers who was renting Mr. Clemens' old bedroom, had worked late into the night arranging his antiques. He was happy with his display. As he left for home he thought his arrangements looked attractive, sure to lure customers.

When he returned the next morning, however, he found all of his furniture and collectibles in the center of the room, pulled away from the walls and stacked in a high pile. He was at first upset and angry to find his previous night's work undone, but when he learned that a ghost had done it, he was more than a little unnerved. Michael is still renting in the Mall, though. He just doesn't do any arranging at night in order not to disturb Mr. Clemens.

On another occasion, Judy, who worked in the Mall, was walking past a display shelf when a lamp fell and hit her on the shoulder. She was well away from the shelf, and there was no explanation—except Mr. Clemens.

Over the years Mr. Clemens has continued to make his presence felt. Items are moved from one stall to another. Displays are rearranged. Lights, which are turned off at night, are on in the morning. Even locked doors and locked showcases are found opened at times.

And no one wants to go upstairs at night. On the second floor are two lamps, which are not on the main circuit breaker and which must be individually turned off each evening. Whoever goes up to do it does not waste any time. They go up, turn the lights off, and then rush back downstairs.

One evening I happened to go to the Mall with a friend. It was closing time and just getting dark. And there was much excitement. I had just missed it. Moments before, one of the dealers had been upstairs rearranging the books in the small stall at the top of the stairs. When she finished, she came right down because of the falling darkness. A couple of minutes later, she and Judy, who was still there, heard a commotion upstairs. Together they went up to the top of the stairs and looked into the stall—a huge pile of books had been stacked in the middle of the room. Judy did not want to go back up and turn out those lights.

Sensing the possibility of an encounter, I volunteered to do it for her. My friend and I walked cautiously up the stairs, went over to the lamps and turned them off. It was almost dusk, and darkness was quickly enveloping the second floor of the building. Only the light from the street lamps outside shone through the windows. The upstairs was all shadow. It was spooky, especially knowing what was up there.

Without saying anything, I motioned for us to sit. At first we just sat there looking at each other, smiling, a bit self-conscious, feeling a little foolish. We sat there for ten minutes. Nothing happened. I was ready to leave when we were suddenly enveloped by a coldness that almost sucked the breath out of us. Together we both jumped up from our seats and tore back down to the light and to Judy. When we told her what had just happened to us, she gave us a worried little smile and quickly ushered us out of the building.

John, David's father-in-law, who sometimes works in the store, said that once recently in the late afternoon when he was getting ready to close, he heard someone walking around upstairs. Thinking a customer was still there, he went up to tell the person the store was closing. When he got up to the top of the stairs, he could see no one, and he walked to the other side of the building so he could look into all of the rooms. There was no one else up there, and the stairs are the only way to the second floor.

Recently, I visited to ask David if I could leave a tape recorder running after the store had closed. He was only too happy to oblige. That evening just before six I returned with my tape recorder, a fresh set of batteries, and a new 120-minute tape. Patsy, one of the dealers, was moving her merchandise from the back corner room, next to Mr. Clemens' bedroom, to another area, so I was enthusiastic and very hopeful that the disruption would spur Mr. Clemens to action. Patsy and I chatted while she rearranged things until David came up to tell us he was closing and to turn off the lights. With great anticipation I turned on the tape recorder, placed it in Mr. Clemens' old room, and said aloud, "Well, Mr. Clemens, you'd sure do me a favor if you'd leave a little something on this recording, kind of let me know you're here." Then we hurried downstairs and out the door.

The next morning when the store opened at eleven I returned to retrieve my recorder. Debbie, who also works there and was opening that morning, met me at the door. Over the years she's had many experiences in the place—articles being moved, strange noises and smells, people walking around upstairs when no one was there—so when she opened the door she wasn't alarmed, but she was breathless. Right before I arrived, she had gone upstairs to turn on the two lamps. When she was about three steps away, both of the lamps came on. That startled her, of course. She looked around and saw no one, but she felt a little uncomfortable, so she turned and started down the stairs. As she was coming down, she felt the presence of someone right behind her, even though she knew she was alone in the building. When she reached the landing, she turned. No one was there.

When I came in, she was very glad to see me. We chatted a few minutes, and then I went upstairs to get my tape recorder. I said goodbye, and, since it was almost noon, walked down to St. George Street to the Mill Top for lunch. I went upstairs and took a table where I could look down on the little courtyard on the north side. It was a beautiful autumn day. Carrie brought me a beer and a Reuben, and I started to rewind the tape.

Now, the tape I was using was a Maxell UR 120. On the face of the cassette at the top there is a space for the label, which I had already added, and right below a thin red line across the face of the cassette. On the left side next to the sprocket is a small red box with "UR" printed in it. On the right side another small red box with "120" in it. About two thirds of the way through the tape as I was rewinding it, the red line and the box with "120" in it began oscillating up and down. Yet the label remained steady, the red box on the other side with "UR" didn't move and the spindles the tape was turning on were not wobbling. I thought I was seeing things. I stopped the tape and called Carrie over. "Look at this," I said and hit the rewind button. The red line and the "120" started oscillating. Carrie looked at it, rolled her eyes, said, "That is too weird," and walked away.

I let the tape rewind all the way and then hit the "play" button. I knew, just knew that Mr. Clemens had left all kinds of stuff for me. I was elated. As I sat there and listened my elation turned to disappointment. Silence. Ten minutes. Twenty minutes. Nothing. But about two thirds of the way through, about the same spot where the line and box had started oscillating, I heard a loud, distinct "click" (pause) "click," "click." It sounded like leather-heeled shoes walking across the floor. I rewound the tape and listened again. Yes, it was definitely someone walking across the wooden floor. I knew no one had been upstairs at the Mall the night before. Was it Mr. Clemens? Finally, I had something that I couldn't explain.

Mr. Clemens may be a little feisty, but he's not a bad ghost. He hasn't done anyone any harm. In fact, Susan and David like having him around. He adds to the antiquity of place, and he certainly provides some excitement.

THE PAINTED

LADY

When I walked in the front door of The Painted Lady Bed and Breakfast I thought I had been transported back a hundred years to the turn of the last century. The plush, dark walls, the exquisite furnishings, the luxuriant atmosphere of the place overwhelmed me. I was equally impressed with Will and Carri Donnan, the owners. They were very easy to talk to and immediately made me feel at home.

Charles Segui, a Minorcan whose ancestors came here in the middle 1700s, built the house in 1910. He was not a wealthy man. He had a bookstore down on St. George Street and also raised carrier pigeons as a hobby. One day a friend of Henry Flagler stopped in Mr. Segui's bookstore. He was a publisher from New York and had heard about Mr. Segui's pigeons. Charley took him to his house and showed the man his pigeons. The publisher bought the entire lot of them and planned to ship them to Cuba to send messages back and forth. Sadly, the ship the pigeons were on sank and all the pigeons were lost. But, luckily for Charley, he had enough money to buy a piece of land in the new Abbott tract, just north of town, and to build the fine Victorian home now known as The Painted Lady.

Apparently, Charley really liked his home—he's still there. He was a very methodical and punctilious man and rode his bicycle back and forth from his store every day at the same time. And every day at two o'clock in the afternoon, he would rush home, run upstairs to change his clothes, and feed his pigeons. Then, he'd change back to his work clothes, come downstairs to eat his lunch, and pedal back to the store. And to this day, precisely at two o'clock the front door will fly open, and a big gray mist will fly upstairs, stomping loudly on the steps. The noise is so loud that the first time it happened, Will, who was back in his workshop, came running out to see what happened. Carri was sitting open-mouthed in the parlor, not believing what she'd just seen and heard. The stairs are carpeted now, but when Charley owned the house the steps were bare wood, and the sound, of course, is his footfalls running up the stairs.

Charley's daughter, Martha Lee, lived in the house until 1989, when she sold it to a couple who turned it into a bed and breakfast. Will and Carri bought it in 2000. During the negotiations, Carri asked if there were any ghosts. The previous owners were evasive. After the closing they did admit, "jewelry occasionally gets played with. There is a playful ghost—but be careful who you tell that to!"

What they didn't know was that Carri was a fourth-generation spiritualist medium. As she put it, "I was born in the hospital and brought home to my grandmother's séance parlor." Will, too, is a practicing medium. They both travel around the world holding seminars and teaching metaphysical classes. So they were both very aware of all the activity taking place in the house.

Their first experience occurred right after they took the over B&B and began renovating. Whenever they went into the back bedroom upstairs in the northeast corner of the house, sorrow would surround them. It was a nondescript room painted a drab green, and they both felt a great sadness when they were in the room. So they began calling it the Sad Room. Carri also felt what she described as a military feeling, a certain stiffness. In any case, the energy was oppressive. After some weeks the Sad Room became the Colonel's Room, because of the military connection Carri felt. And so it remained for several months. Whenever Carri went into the room she began itching as if she was wearing a wool uniform with all the buttons buttoned.

One day Carri, in a whimsical mood, decided to paint the Colonel's Room pink, a very feminine "foo-foo" pink, as Carri put it, and she put a flower border around the walls. The sadness immediately went away. It became a happy room. In fact, when Carri and Will showed me the room, I could feel the happiness, but it's still called the Colonel's Room.

The year after, when the room had long been renamed the Colonel's Room, Carri and Will happened to be talking to Giselle next door at Le Pavillon, and Carri asked her about the people who had built the house. She had heard that the old lady the previous owners had bought the house from had been a spinster. She was curious.

"You're right, Carri. Martha Lee was the daughter of the original owner, and she had been an old maid until the day she died. She was around eighty-nine, I think. Never had a boyfriend. Never dated. Never married. She had a sad story. When she was in her twenties, her father died, and she and her mother, Maude, had to take in boarders to make ends meet. Well, one of the boarders was this man, very handsome, I guess. They put him in the back corner

35

bedroom, the one that opens onto the back porch. The story goes that Martha Lee soon fell in love with him, and one day Maude caught them together in a compromising position in Martha Lee's room, which also opens on the same back porch, as you know. Well, puritanical old Maude was outraged. It was the 1940s, so you can imagine. She threw the man out of the house and told him never to come back. Apparently, he moved to California, and Martha Lee never saw him again. She mourned for him the rest of her life."

"That is sad," Carri said. "What was the man's name?"

Giselle replied, "You know, that's funny. Martha Lee never called him by name 'til the day she died. All she ever said was that the only true love of her life was 'the colonel.'"

Carri and Will were dumbstruck. Not knowing the story, they had been calling the bedroom the Colonel's Room for months.

After they had shown me the Colonel's Room and told me the story about the colonel and Martha Lee, they led me out onto the back porch and into Martha Lee's Room. It was beautiful, with a four-poster canopy bed, wonderful oil paintings on the walls, and fine Victorian furniture.

"It's the most haunted room in the B&B," Carri explained, "and the most popular. There are all kinds of stories about this room. See that oil painting," pointing to the painting at the head of the queen-sized canopy bed of a beautiful young woman wearing a Victorian dress and a huge Victorian hat. "That's in honor of Martha Lee. Beautiful, huh? Well, some people actually call her the 'other lady of the house.' They bring presents for her, and all these hats hanging around here have been left by guests to honor Martha Lee.

"And I have to tell you a funny story. Lots of times when no one else is in the house and Will and I are downstairs, we'll hear this bed squeaking. We always laugh. We tell each other that old Maude isn't around anymore, so Martha Lee and the colonel are up here together again. And there are people who believe that Martha Lee casts love spells on couples in this room. They say when they're in this bed, they feel someone pushing them together. They say if you're having marital problems, just come and stay in Martha Lee's room! Isn't that funny? Then, there're the doors that open and shut, and the doorknobs that turn. People are always seeing stuff like that. And we've had many people who feel Martha Lee pulling the covers up and tucking them in at night."

Carri had another funny story to tell me. Some really weird guests, complete with spiked hair, came to spend the night. They were in St. Augustine for a wedding and were running late, so Carri and Will checked them in and took them up to Martha Lee's Room, where they just dropped their bags and left for the wedding. They didn't return until about eleven that night and had to be in Jacksonville at seven the next morning to catch a plane. So they were only in the room from eleven until six. When Will went up to clean the room the next morning the heavy oil painting of Martha Lee was turned upside down. The couple could have played a little joke on Carri and Will, but they didn't think so. They were only in the room a short time, and they had to have been tired. No, Carri thinks Martha Lee was just not too pleased to have them in her room.

Because the B&B is so haunted, many paranormal research groups come through. In fact, not long ago, a big group came in to do research on several locations and stayed at The Painted Lady. One man in the team was rather macho and arrogant. He had heard stories about the B&B and wanted Martha to scare him. Carri told him to be careful about what he wished for, then checked him in and showed him up to Martha Lee's Room.

A few minutes after Carri got downstairs, she heard a crash, and the man came storming down. He was incensed. He had sat on the bed and it collapsed. "What kind of cheap beds do you have in this place, anyway?" he asked. Will assured him that the beds were not cheap, that most of them were antiques. Hundreds of people had slept in the bed in that room, and it had never before fallen apart. Carri warned him again about not wishing for things he wasn't prepared to handle. Then, Will went up and put the bed back together, tightened everything and straightened the slats under the box springs. Not five minutes later, the bed crashed down again.

This time when the man came down he was really angry. "Scared yet?" Carri asked him.

"I'm not scared. I'm mad. I'm not sleeping on that cheap bed. I want another room."

They moved him over to the Colonel's Room, and everything went well the rest of the afternoon. Later that night, long after Will and Carri had gone to bed, someone started pounding on the front door. Will got up and answered it. It was the arrogant guy from the Colonel's Room. He was in his pajamas, and his feet were bare. And he wasn't so arrogant.

"Now I'm scared," he said. "I just went out on the back porch to have a cigarette before going to bed, and the door slammed shut. Locked on me. I couldn't get back in."

That door doesn't lock without a key. The key was in the room, and no one else was there. Carri again chided the man about wishing for supernatural experiences. He began apologizing to her, but she said, "Don't apologize to me. Apologize to Martha Lee. Tell her you're sorry. You know she's there. Be a little more respectful." He did, and the rest of the weekend went by without incident.

Carri had another Martha Lee story for me. Martha Lee had a cat, a big orange tabby named Toby. She had him for eighteen years. He died before Martha Lee sold the house, but he's still around. He's the most frequently seen ghost here. Will and Carri see him out of the corner of their eyes in several different places in the house. He wanders all over the neighborhood, and neighbors still see him. There's an elderly lady who lives in the house right behind The Painted Lady parking lot who sees him all the time. Guests will hear a cat meowing inside the house, and Carri and Will don't own a cat.

Carri pointed to the daybed in Martha Lee's Room. "See that daybed? Well, innkeepers like things nice and tidy and like the bed-spreads to be tight and smooth. At least, I do. When I come up to clean this room, I'll always smooth that daybed out. When we first got the place I'd come in here, make the beds and clean up, and I would always smooth the daybed out. Then, if I came back up in the middle of the day, I'd always find an indentation right in the middle of it, and I'd say, 'Will, stop playing jokes,' because I'd think that he'd come in and made those indentations. One Monday I was cleaning up, making beds, and such. Will had gone to the grocery store, and no one else was in the house. I had made the bed—and straightened the daybed—and had gone out to get fresh towels. When I came back in, there was the indentation. We found out later all about Toby from the neighbors. He still comes in here a lot, only now he also gets on the bed." We all laughed at that.

Carri had one final story about Martha Lee. Recently, one of the many paranormal research groups came to The Painted Lady to study voice phenomena and take orb photos. The group started in the gift shop taking photos and recording sounds, asking for confir-mation, saying things like, "If there are any spirits in here please make your presence felt." When they had fully explored the gift shop they moved upstairs. Carri followed them around but didn't hear or sense a thing. She is clairvoyant and very aware of all the paranormal activity that goes on around the B&B. Neither she nor Will sensed anything during the group's tour of the house.

When the research group finally finished, they all went into the parlor to listen to what they had captured on the tape recorder. Carri was sure they weren't going to hear anything, because neither she nor Will had heard or sensed anything clairvoyantly. Well, she was shocked.

On the recording as one of the team was asking for any spirits to make their presence known, a lady with a Southern drawl cut in and said, 'Git outta here, dadburn it!' just as loud as you please. 'Git outta here, dadburn it.' Carri almost fainted, because neither Will nor she had heard or even sensed anything. Carri thought it was Martha Lee and that she was displeased with all the people and equipment there. She just wanted everyone to 'git outta here, dadburn it!' Will and Carri got a kick out of that.

On that same visit, research photographers got some excellent orb shots. Orbs are those little balls of light you sometimes see in photos that you can't explain. Some people think they're actually spirits, but Carri and Will don't. They think they are just places through which spirit energy enters and exits. In the far corner of what used to be their bedroom in the back of the gift shop, they had a small chair. The photographs captured a cluster of orbs that started over the chair in the back corner of the gift shop, ran up through the ceiling into the room above, and right through the ceiling up there. And in that corner both downstairs and in the room above, Carri and Will experience all kinds of phenomena. It's a very active area.

Carri thought of something else. "Oh, Will, tell him about that group of women."

Will smiled. "Yes, we had six women from a paranormal society staying here not long ago. They had been out ghost hunting around town and on their way back to the B&B around midnight, they passed the Huguenot Cemetery, and as they passed one of them said, 'If there's anyone there, come on and party with us.' They came back, went upstairs, and congregated in that room above our old bedroom before going to bed. They were just sitting there talking, when this specter appeared out of nowhere. He was a small man dressed in a Victorian era suit. He was very pleasant and polite and even introduced himself. You can imagine the ladies were a little shocked. He stayed there talking to them for a few minutes, looked around, and said, 'This isn't a party.' And he evaporated into thin air. And all six of them said they saw and talked to him."

I had to change tapes in my recorder, so there was a short lull in the conversation, but as soon as I snapped the cover shut, Carri started in again. "And I have to tell you about our beloved Eleanor."

"Eleanor?" I asked.

"Yes, Eleanor. She was our sweet old dog, a Rhodesian ridgeback."

They named her Eleanor after Carri's aunt, who had Rhodesian ridgebacks. And Carri's aunt was named after Eleanor Roosevelt, so indirectly the canine Eleanor was named after Mrs. Roosevelt. Carri and Will had her for years, but eventually Elie got old and arthritic with tumors all over her body. All she could do was sit in the big old chair in the dining room. Finally, one day around Christmas, Will decided that she was suffering too much and took her to the vet to be put to sleep.

Carri was devastated. She cried and cried while Will was gone, but when he came home and opened the door, her spirits brightened. She could just feel Elie with him. And Eleanor didn't feel old and decrepit. She was young and full of energy, and her tail was wagging. It was very comforting.

And her energy remained. Elie went nuts over chicken, just loved it. Even now, when Carri cooks chicken, Elie's right there thumping her tail on the floor. And she loved to go to the beach.

41

When they go to the beach now, Carri feels the dog getting into the car. Her presence is very reassuring.

Carri wasn't finished. "Now we had this man, Gary, who came in off the street to get an aura photo done—I'll tell you about aura photos in a minute. Anyway, he seemed a bit skeptical. When I read his photo, I could see a spirit face in it, and I told him that I saw the face of a man who been a prisoner of war with him, but he had died in the POW camp. Well, Gary was floored. 'How did you know that?' He was really shook up. He started coming over often, although he was still a bit skeptical. He came over one day and started to sit in Eleanor's chair. I said, 'Wait a minute, Gary, Eleanor is in that chair. Tell her to get out first.' He gave me this sheepish grin and said, 'Yeah, right. Sure she is.' So I said, 'Come on, Elie, Gary wants to sit in the chair.' And immediately the cushion, which had been compressed, came back up. Gary jumped back and stared at that chair. That's when he became a believer."

Carri then changed the topic and began talking about aura photos. She explained that all living things have an electromagnetic energy surrounding them, which gives them a unique representation of their spiritual, emotional, physical, and mental well being. The Russians developed "Kirlian photography" that captures this energy on film, and the Japanese have created a more sophisticated adaptation. The method involves high frequency electric currents, and light vibrating at different frequencies shows up on film as different colors, so an aura photo will show the image of whomever or whatever is being photographed with all these colors around them. Will takes the photo, and Carri interprets it.

She went on, "One day a couple came in off the street wanting an aura photo. Will took the picture and when I sat down with them to interpret the colors, I got this message to tell them Lily was here. I asked if any of them knew a Lily, because there was a spirit energy in the photo and she kept telling me to tell them that Lily was here. Well, when I said that, they started giggling. Finally, they asked if anyone had called and told me about their coming over. I said no one had, and they then told me they were staying at the St. Francis Inn. I still didn't get it, so one woman said, 'You know, the St. Francis has a ghost named Lily, and just before we came over here, we were talking to some of the other guests and were saying that it would be funny if Lily came with us and got her picture taken, too.' And I said, 'Well, there she is.'" (NOTE: The story of Lily and the St. Francis Inn is included in *Ghosts of St. Augustine*, Pineapple Press, 1997.)

I was a bit incredulous, but Carri assured me, "I swear. This is absolutely 100 percent true."

Will ended the conversation. "As you can see, this building is only two stories. Recently, we had a couple staying in Martha Lee's Room. In the middle of the night the woman woke her husband up and complained that the people upstairs were making too much noise. The husband smiled, 'Go back to sleep, love. There is no upstairs.' Things like that happen often, but, except for the guy who wanted to be scared, no one has ever had any bad experiences. In fact, all our guests say they feel protected and surrounded by love, like they were being watched over."

And who wouldn't feel that way with Martha Lee tucking you in at night?

HOST TOUR

*L*ou was a tough New Jersey cop. He had retired from the police force a short time before he met Barbara on the Internet. They corresponded daily for several months and soon became good friends, so Barbara invited Lou to visit her in St. Augustine. They met, and their friendship quickly became love. Lou also fell in love with St. Augustine. So, with few ties in New Jersey and much beckoning in the Ancient City, Lou moved down, and he and Barbara were married.

Not long after he came to Florida, Lou took a job as a tour guide for a local tour company, driving one of the trains on a historic motorized tour of the city. Of course, he had to study St. Augustine history, get a guide's license, and learn the script for the tour. The standards for guides in St. Augustine are quite high. They must "know" the city, as well as the sites on their tours, in great detail. Becoming a St. Augustine tour guide is not an easy thing to do. And with Lou, who knew little about the city, or even Florida for that matter, there was the added burden of over-coming his New Jersey accent. "Youse guys wit dis n' dat" is not acceptable among St. Augustine tour guides.

Lou studied very hard and soon could answer just about any question anyone could throw at him concerning St. Augustine. And he practiced his script, endlessly going over it and repeating each word time and again to wipe out all traces of his Yankee tongue. Barbara helped, too. She and her two grown children listened to Lou give his tour and critiqued him word by word. Slowly, his accent disappeared, and he got to know his tour so well, he never had to even glance at the script in his guide's handbook. He was almost ready.

One day Lou went to his boss to tell him how well he was doing and that he would soon be able to start giving tours. His boss suggested that he go out in the evening after the traffic died down, and drive his route in his car, speaking the tour script into a tape recorder. He could then take the tape home to play and review.

That evening about nine o'clock Lou got into his car with a small handheld tape recorder, new batteries, and a fresh tape, and drove to the Old Jail on San Marcos, where the tour began. At the Old Jail, he put the batteries and the new tape into his tape recorder and closed his eyes to visualize himself in the driver's seat of a train with thirty or forty people sitting expectantly behind him. He took a deep breath, put his imaginary train in gear, and started his spiel for the enraptured tourists on his train.

Traffic was light, as it usually is in St. Augustine after nine o'clock. But this night was a cold February mid-week evening, and there were few cars on the road. Lou quickly got into his talk and was very comfortable with it. Soon he was heading south past the Castillo and the bay on his left, the inns and other points of inter-est on his right. The Old Market. The Cathedral. The Government

House. Lou felt as if he had been doing this forever. On he went, back and forth across town, continuing south, and finally swinging back north. Before he knew it, he found himself at the Fountain of Youth and was almost at the end of the tour. At the northwest corner of the Fountain of Youth at the intersection of Dufferin and Magnolia he pointed out the tabby wall which surrounds the attraction, explained the difference between tabby, which is a concrete made from oyster shells, and coquina, a sedimentary rock used to build the Castillo. Then he turned left on Dufferin, headed out to San Marcos Avenue, and drove back down to the Old Jail. He was quite pleased with himself. He was ready for a real tour.

It was almost eleven when Lou arrived back home. Barbara was still awake, reading in bed. They briefly talked about listening to the tape then but decided against it, preferring to wait until morning, when they could give it their full attention and her kids could be there to hear it also.

The next day the four of them sat down to critique the tape. Lou was proud of himself, and, indeed, as they listened they had very little criticism and nothing very significant. Towards the end of the tape as Lou pointed out the Fountain of Youth and began explaining the difference between tabby and coquina, they were all pleased for Lou, because he had given a really good tour.

Suddenly, in the middle of his tabby and coquina explanation, his voice stopped—and was replaced by a horrible, unearthly noise! All four of them jerked up in their chairs, goose bumps on their arms, their hair bristling. The dog scampered out of the room. The sound coming from the tape recorder was ghastly.

There were several voices, at least two, maybe three, all talking at the same time. One of the voices was unintelligible. It was a deep voice, perhaps a male, speaking so slowly it could not be understood. It sounded as if the person were in a great deal of pain. A second voice, a woman's, was whispering in French. She could be understood. " . . . Ne fais pas ça . . . " " . . . Don't do that . . ." " . . . Je peux t'excuser . . . mon cher, enfin, chut, chut, je peux t'excuser . . ." "I can forgive you . . . my dear, after all, hush, hush. I can forgive you." She went on and on. Then she talked about a box. "You are going to drop the box. You are going to drop the box." After more of what appeared to be only half of a conversation between two people she said, "J'y vais, adieu, adieu, au revoir." "I'm leaving, so long, so long, goodbye." And finally she finished, "My spirit without them . . . "

There were other almost inaudible whisperings superimposed on these two voices. There was also a sound vaguely like a chain being dragged over cobblestones, or rapid finger-tapping on a small drum, smaller than a bongo, or even water lapping against a boat. It was a quick, uneven, indescribable rapping sound. The unnerving noise continued for four or five minutes to the end of the tape.

Lou, Barbara, and her two children sat motionless, stunned. What had they just heard? Could that have been real? They were petrified. Finally Lou got up, went across the room to the stereo, rewound the tape a bit, and played the last part again. Again Lou's voice stopped and the unearthly noises started. They played the tape several more times that day, and gradually overcame their fear, but to this day they have yet to overcome their wonder.

Lou made several copies of the end of the tape to see if anyone could explain the unearthly noises. It has been almost five years since the incident, and no one has come up with an explanation. Nothing else untoward has happened to Lou and Barbara in that time either. Soon after this phenomenon, Lou began conducting tours, which he is still doing to this day.

Somewhere in the vicinity of the Fountain of Youth a burial ground once existed. No one is sure of the exact location. Then, too,

St. Augustine's past has often been chaotic and violent. Perhaps the French woman was soothing a dying man, and Lou's tape recorder just happened to catch these whispers on the wind from another time. Whatever the sounds were, Lou is exceedingly happy that he hasn't heard them since.

ERBAL

CREATIONS

M ost of the buildings along San Marco Avenue north of the Castillo are newer than those farther south, since the area was outside the city walls and more subject to the vagaries of marauding French, English, and Indians. Still, San Marco has its own history and its own stories. Today most of the private homes have been turned into commercial enterprises, and the area has become known for its numerous antique stores and quaint shops.

One such shop is Herbal Creations at 39 San Marco Avenue. Built in 1860, it is owned by a delightful and spunky lady, Hollie Criswell, who has filled it with herbs, incense, and candles and has developed a wonderful garden outside. It is calm and peaceful, a place of refuge. Hollie describes her shop as "creating a garden for the senses."

A friend told me about this interesting little shop with strange happenings, so I went to visit Hollie. The atmosphere of the shop is tranquil, especially the former front bedroom upstairs, which Hollie has made into a meditation room for customers. She showed me around the store, upstairs and down, then escorted me to a pleasant spot in the garden outside. Every inch of space is well tended and given to herbs and flowers, fountains and sculptures, all designed to promote peace and tranquility. When we were comfortably settled, she began her story.

"When I first moved into the house, I was upstairs watering plants and those little fountains. I felt something soft rub against my legs—I was wearing shorts and my legs were bare. I looked down to see what it was, but there was nothing there. I couldn't figure it out. At the time, I just shrugged it off, but it went on for weeks. And then Judy, who worked for me, had the same thing happen to her. Neither of us had a clue as to what it was. Never ever imagined it was a ghost or anything.

"Sometime later, a friend of mine brought over her new husband to introduce him to me. He happened to be involved in paranormal studies of some kind, so I told him about our experiences. He immediately smiled this knowing smile.

"It turned out to be a cat. Imagine that! A ghost cat! It was sort of comforting."

Might this cat have been Martha Lee's Toby from up the street at the Painted Lady? Toby was a tom and given to roaming. Several of the neighbors have seen him roving about the neighborhood.

There's also an older lady there. The pharmacist at Eckerd's, Hollie's friend, told her that he knew the lady who lived in the house for a long time. Sweet woman, very nice to everyone. After she had died and Hollie had bought the place, he came over and gave her a picture of the woman. Months later an elderly lady came in and said, "I just had to come in here and see what you'd done to this place, because my husband's mother used to live here. She was a sweet old lady. Always dressed nice and wore her hair in a bun."

Hollie related, "At that point I remembered the picture, and I dug it out and handed it to her. She got teary-eyed and said, 'Yes, that's her,' so I gave her the picture.

"Later, there was a customer and her twelve-year-old daughter who've been regulars for a long time. They came in one day, she looked at me, and she asked, 'You know you have a ghost in here, don't you?'

"I answered, 'Why, I've heard I have one,' and I smiled because I was thinking of the cat.

"'Well,' my friend said, 'she's an elderly lady with her hair in a bun.' That surprised me because I'd never heard about any ghosts other than the cat.

"Then I said, 'You're kidding. Where did you see her?'

"She replied, 'Why, right next to you at the cash register. She's standing there right now.'"

Hollie was astonished. She looked around, startled. But, of course, she didn't see anything. She never sees anything. In fact, the cat is the only thing she's ever been aware of, although others from time to time come in and see both the cat and the lady.

We chatted for a while and went back inside to look around again. Finally, I thanked her and said goodbye.

I returned several days later with my friend and ghost chaser, Joanne. As soon as we walked in the door, the hair on Joanne's arms stood up, as it always does when she encounters anything. She looked at her arms, then at me with a little smirk. I could tell she wasn't alarmed or frightened by whatever she was feeling. I introduced her to Hollie. After we exchanged pleasantries, Joanne wandered off to look around, and I got into a conversation with Hollie. After a while, I saw Joanne climb the stairs to the second floor. Hollie and I went on with our conversation.

Some time later, at least twenty minutes, I wondered where Joanne was. She had been upstairs a long time. I mentioned it to Hollie, and she suggested we go up and see.

The stairs go from the front of the house on the ground floor to the back upstairs. There is a hallway, which leads to the two front rooms. We went down the hall and looked into the meditation room. Joanne was sitting there in a rocking chair. She looked up at us as we entered and smiled.

Hollie smiled back, "I guess you like my room, huh?"

Joanne laughed, "Yes, I do. It's really peaceful in here, but let me tell you what just happened."

I could see it coming. Joanne had experienced something.

Joanne stopped rocking. "I walked up the stairs, and when I got to the top I turned to go down the hall. There was a woman in front of me—I hadn't seen her coming up, and I didn't see her until I turned. She was walking down the hall also, so maybe she'd come from one of the back rooms. Anyway, I had wanted to come in here and see what this room was like, but she came in first and sat down in this chair. Well, I didn't want to disturb her, so I went into the other room to check out all the incense. I was in there a long time, and I wanted to get into the meditation room, so after several minutes I went to the doorway and glanced in. I expected to see the woman still sitting there, because I hadn't seen or heard her leave. Well, guess what? The room was empty. Not a soul! That's when I came in and sat down."

Hollie and I looked at each other. We hadn't seen anyone come down the stairs either. "What'd she look like, Joanne?"

"Funny. She had on a kind of old-fashioned housedress like my grandmother used to wear and slippers. Oh, and she was elderly. Gray hair done up in a bun. That reminded me of my grandmother a little, too."

Hollie and I laughed, and I said, "Maybe she just came up to look for her cat. At least she's not hanging out at the cash register."

In any case, Hollie's gentle ghosts nicely complement the serene atmosphere of Herbal Creations.

I dropped by recently and Michelle, who works for Hollie, was there. We chatted briefly and I asked her if anything strange had been happening.

It had. Just the other day something creepy occurred. Normally, when Michelle closes up, she looks upstairs to make sure no one is still in the shop, then comes down, turns things off, locks up, and goes home. On this particular day, she did just that, but as she was headed for the front door to leave, something made her go back upstairs. It was really compelling, as if something were forcing her to go up.

"I went right to the back room. There is a door back there, which is always locked, so I never even check it usually. Anyway, I went right to that door, almost against my will, and—would you believe it—the door was unlocked. It's never unlocked. I think what happened was that someone had gone up earlier and unlocked it in order to rob the place later in the evening. I guess our ghost is really an angel looking out for us."

C ASTLE WARDEN

Castle Warden—Ripley's Believe It or Not! Museum—is an imposing structure, especially considering it was built originally as a one-family house. Barbara Golden, Ripley's director of sales and marketing, met me in the Cargo Hold Gift Shop for my own private tour of the museum on San Marco Avenue. She was a very pleasant lady who didn't seem at all inconvenienced by being taken away from her busy schedule. I was receiving her full and undivided attention. We left the gift shop and headed down the arcade to the front entrance where she began to tell me all about this unique place.

Built in 1887 by William Warden, a millionaire businessman from the Northeast and partner with Henry Flagler and John D. Rockefeller in Standard Oil Company, Castle Warden was the winter residence for his family of sixteen. It was designed and built by Carriere and Hastings, the same firm that constructed Henry Flagler's Ponce de Leon and Alcazar Hotels at the south end of town. The original mansion had nineteen bedrooms on the three main floors for the family and five for the servants in the North wing. White Italian marble covered the floor and steps of the first level, with beautiful hardwood floors in the main hall and upper levels. An enormous, exquisite leaded stained-glass skylight towered above the main hall, and black Vermont marble filled the many fireplaces. Castle Warden was a masterpiece.

The Wardens lived there until the last member of the family, Elizabeth Warden Ketterlinus, and her husband, John, moved in 1925. Then Castle Warden stood vacant and boarded up for sixteen years, a haven for vagrants, until Norton Baskin and his wife, Marjorie Kinnan Rawlings, the famous Florida writer and Pulitzer Prize-winning author of *The Yearling*, bought the mansion in 1941 and rehabilitated it as the Castle Warden Hotel. It opened in April 1942 with twenty-five guest rooms. Many prominent literary and political figures were regular visitors.

Fire struck the hotel one Sunday morning in April 1944, while Mr. Baskin was off fighting in World War II and Ms. Rawlings was at her cottage in Cross Creek. A haphazardly dropped cigarette was the probable cause of the fire. It was contained on the third and fourth floors, but two guests died of smoke inhalation. Mrs. Ruth Hopkins Pickering, a woman in her early forties and a close friend of Ms. Rawlings, was staying in Ms. Rawlings' penthouse. She was found in her night attire on the floor of her bathroom. And Miss Betty Nevi Richeson, a young Jacksonville socialite in her twenties, was found in her bathtub directly below Mrs. Pickering. Apparently, both women had tried to save themselves from the deadly fumes and heat with wet towels. One of the hotel bellboys, who tried to get to the women, heard Mrs. Pickering screaming from a window, but was unable to reach either of them because of the flames. Firemen who eventually reached the rooms found signs of intense heat but no actual burns on either body. The hotel reopened within weeks, but Baskin sold it in 1946 and it remained a hotel until 1948.

Robert Ripley, often called "The Modern Marco Polo," was a frequent visitor to Castle Warden and had tried repeatedly and unsuccessfully to buy it to display his vast collection of oddities and curios. Shortly after his death in 1949, his heirs were able to purchase the then-closed hotel and convert it into the first permanent Ripley's Believe It or Not! Museum.

As we started up the broad staircase to walk through all the rooms to view some of the 750 exhibits, Barbara explained, "There's a lot of crazy stuff that goes on in here, nothing bad, just spooky. I'm a little skeptical myself, but we've had so many people see and hear things, and so many paranormal research teams have been through here, it's hard not to believe. We ask investigators here about once a year, but I think we'll stop that, because it seems to just stir things up. A lot of people walk through the building and hear stringed instruments playing where there is no music at all. It's like a symphony orchestra or string quartet. And we had several people who heard what sounded like a child plunking on a piano as well as someone playing a concert piano. I asked Carri Donnan, the medium up the street, who owns The Painted Lady B&B, to come down and see what she thought. She said it was a piano teacher teaching children to play the piano and another person, a concert pianist, who just couldn't get enough and played at every opportunity. Then, there was the mother of one of the ghost-tour guides who came along on the tour. She knew nothing of the music, and she reported hearing a harp being played.

"There are times when you hear things moving on the second floor and you know there's no one up there and everything is turned off. We used to have an exhibit called Wax Hands, and it was interactive. There was one man who worked here and said one day that he was working up near that exhibit when he felt somebody come up and pull on his belt. There wasn't a soul around.

"We also have some objects that I wonder might have had something brought in with them, like a voodoo doll, which belonged to Papa Doc Duvalier, the former infamous dictator of Haiti. You just wonder what kind of baggage is attached to that. It's totally harmless, but you feel . . . there are times when I walk through here and I know absolutely that someone's walking along with me. When Carri came in, she didn't even know about the voodoo doll, but as soon as she came up on the second floor she heard drums beating and asked, 'Is there something to do with voodoo up here in this room? It's real apparent to me.' She was not fifteen feet away from that doll. But I came up here the other day, picked the doll up, and didn't feel a thing.

"And there're the lights. Once we had some paranormal investigators coming in after the ghost tour went through, after closing. The lobby lights and the TV that shows an instructional video there are all on the same breaker, and as they were preparing, they flipped the breaker off to turn off the lights—the TV went off and then came right back on. Tell me how that happened. They had a lot of activity that night, photographs of orbs with contrails all over the place, and readings on their electromagnetic meters.

"There's a lot of activity in the gift shop, too. Things get moved all the time. You know, the manager and the people who work in there are so meticulous. They always want displays to look exactly right. It's a really nice gift shop. Before they close at night someone always goes around straightening up and putting things away. Then, the next morning, they'll find key chains hung in bizarre places, shirts flipped over.

"And our maintenance people when they come in, in the morning, some are a little apprehensive when they walk through turning on lights and opening things up. But it's not a major thing. The spirits are here. They're peaceful. We come in, in the morning and say hello, let them know we're here."

Last year Barbara asked Sandy Craig of Tour St. Augustine to bring a team through. Sandy brought along two of her tour guides, Dawn and Susan, as well as Elaine and my friend and sensitive ghost chaser, Joanne.

As they ascended the stairs from the lobby, Joanne suddenly experienced the empathetic symptoms of a bent, old woman, an octogenarian with severe osteoporosis, who was having trouble climbing the stairs above the landing. As Joanne walked up she suddenly felt very, very tired, and it took a great deal of effort to move up each step. She began to bend forward until she was bent almost 90° with her face looking down at her feet. At the same time she received the impression of a very old woman with short, white hair and a severely bent back, grasping the railing as she (and Joanne) labored up each step. They were walking in the same place at the same time, and Joanne was empathetically copying her actions. Joanne didn't feel any anxiety or fear, just the weariness of old age. "Poor lady," she thought. "I wish she would discover the elevator." Oddly, she never seemed to be aware of Joanne's presence.

When they got to the top of the stairs, they entered the display room immediately to the west of the main hall, which houses the huge Erector Set Ferris Wheel. The display room and the corner room just south of it had been bedrooms when the building was a hotel. As soon as Joanne entered, she was seized with fear and panic. She did not want to enter that room. Just inside the doorway she experienced shortness of breath and coldness, and she encountered a strong, negative energy that she quickly recognized as a female ghost in her mid-40s wearing a plain, green dress and with short, curled dark blond or ash brown hair. At first she interpreted the energy as anger but then realized that this spirit was trying to protect her from some danger, like a parent pulling a child from the path of an oncoming car. She did not want Joanne to go into that smaller room.

Finally, at Sandy's request and when it became apparent that the ghost was not going to follow her, Joanne entered. She gasped for breath and became very dizzy. "I can't breathe," she exclaimed and began staggering around the room in a counter-clockwise direction as if she were caught up in some sort of invisible whirlwind. She felt like she was enveloped by thick gray smoke swirling around her. (At this point she had been told nothing about the history of the building, neither the fire nor the deaths. She purposely avoids learning anything about an area she is going to enter, so that her impressions are not tainted.) She did not feel any heat or sense any fire, only the swirling thick smoke. She felt as if she was going to black out, so she stepped into the other room and sat next to the window. No sooner had she sat down than the lady in the green dress once again tried to force her back out to the hallway.

Since she wasn't going to have any peace in the big display room either, Joanne went back into the other room where she was immediately caught up in the vortex of swirling smoke and began staggering around. Her symptoms of shortness of breath increased and she thought her lungs would burst, but she felt no pain, only a loss of breath and panic. All this time the rest of Sandy's team stood there watching Joanne. None of them were affected.

Suddenly, for Joanne, all the movement stopped, and she was surrounded by intense silence and a deep cold, a cold that began in her core and moved outward in her body, which felt as heavy as stone. She forced herself to move but felt as if she was dragging her legs through mud. Moments earlier when she was caught up in the vortex of smoke, she was thinking of rescue. Now her concern was only to be seen. She had the feeling that she was dead and invisible. She was overcome with sorrow and hopeless despair as the team stood frozen, aghast. She kept yelling, "It's so cold. Can't anyone feel the cold?" Finally, she staggered out of the room, collapsed against the wall, and sat for several minutes, because she was shaking so violently. Elaine got a sweater for her. After several minutes, her symptoms began to fade and she was able to stand and continue the investigation.

As Joanne later said, "I have never before had an experience like this. I absolutely believe that I empathetically experienced the panic, suffocation from smoke and sudden spirit entrapment of at least one Caucasian female. I also feel that the female ghost in the larger room was actually trying to protect me."

"I feel this is an actual, ongoing haunting which is the result of traumatic memories and feelings of someone who suffered and died from smoke inhalation. Perhaps Mrs. Pickering tried to prevent me from entering the 'vortex room' to save me from suffocating. Due to my experience in that room, I continue to argue that, regardless of where history records that the bodies were actually found, a woman or women suffocated violently from smoke inhalation in that particular room. Perhaps Betty crawled, choking, from that room into her bathroom."

It was several minutes before they could continue on. When they did they encountered a glassed-in display surrounded by an iron pike fence about three feet high. Joanne impulsively reached across the fence with her right hand and was surprised to feel a strong, electric shock that hit the palm of her hand and traveled up her arm. "Wow! There's some kind of laser beam alarm here, I guess." Sandy replied that there wasn't, and Elaine pointed out that a little boy in a visiting school group had tried to jump over the fence and been impaled. The boy lived but the offending pike had been removed. Joanne looked down and noticed that, sure enough, the pike was gone.

When they entered the theater room, which was the location of the bathroom where Betty Richardson's body was found in 1944, Joanne felt nothing, at least nothing from the fire. She did say that, "We encountered a friendly, if curious, adult male ghost who enjoyed following us around." He was a dapper man, about six feet tall, thin, with short, dark hair and dressed in a dark, pinstriped suit. He was especially attracted to Susan and followed her closely. She asked him if he liked the group—mostly females. Her electromagnetic meter flashed brightly. When she asked him if he'd like them to leave, the meter was blank. This guy seemed to really enjoy flirting with women. He was harmless and quite nice, actually. Joanne suspected him of being the cause of any poltergeist tricks, especially to unsuspecting women.

After spending some time in the theater, and flirting with Mr. Dapper, the group went on without incident. Later, in the parking lot Dawn happened to turn on her meter and pointed it toward Joanne. It lit up like the Fourth of July. "Oh, oh, Joanne," Dawn laughed. "Somebody is following you home."

Joanne was not amused. She sensed that it was Mr. Dapper, and she yelled at him, "No, you are not allowed to follow me. Go back inside!" Dawn's meter went dead.

Barbara and I finished our tour too, and she escorted me back outside. As we said goodbye Barbara reminded me, "You know, we've never had any trouble here. It's educational and a fun place to visit." I couldn't agree with her more. In fact, although I don't have any grandchildren of my own, I sure have a lot of young friends, and we're coming back. They'll love this fascinating castle.

CASA DE LA PAZ

Casa de la Paz Bayfront Bed and Breakfast is one of the finest B&Bs in St. Augustine. My wife and I have stayed there, and it is truly a peaceful place. Built in 1915 by Mr. J. Duncan Puller, a local banker, it has served as private residence, restaurant, school, apartment building, and finally as an inn.

Harry and his wife, Brenda, bought the then-vacant building in 1984 and spent two years renovating it, doing much of the work themselves. When they first began spending time there, working or supervising workmen, nothing seemed amiss. But soon they began to hear things, most often footsteps up and down the hallway on the second floor and on the staircase. Neither thought much about it, attributing the noise to workmen or to each other.

Then, one night after everyone else had left, Harry, who was upstairs, called down and said he was going to take out some trash and then they could leave. Brenda was in the dining room. Several minutes later, she heard footsteps on the staircase and a swishing noise.

"Harry, what are you doing up there?" she yelled. "I thought you were taking out trash," and she stepped out of the dining room into the hall and looked up the stairs—right into the face of a pretty young woman, dressed in a black suit with a black, brimmed hat and a small suitcase. Brenda stopped, stunned. She started to say something when the young woman disappeared before her eyes.

Brenda was so startled, she raced out the back door all the way to Charlotte Street behind the building. Harry was there, stacking up pieces of broken wood to be hauled off.

"What's the matter with you, Brenda. You look like you've seen a ghost."

Brenda was out of breath and gasped, "I . . . I have seen a ghost. There's a ghost in that house, Harry."

Harry laughed, "You need a rest, sweetheart."

"No, I'm serious. I just saw the ghost of a young woman on the staircase," and she described what had happen. "Those footsteps we've been hearing must be her walking up and down the hallway."

Harry didn't question his wife but found it hard to believe. However, as the weeks and months passed, they heard and saw the young woman many times. By the time they had completed their renovation and opened the bed and breakfast, she was just part of the scenery.

In 1986 Harry and Brenda held an open house and invited all their friends to celebrate the completion of renovations and the opening of the B&B. At one point Harry and two friends, Page and Alan, were talking in the hall with their backs to the staircase. Another friend, Gay, and her husband, Danny, were sitting on a sofa along the south wall of the living room. The place was packed and noisy.

Gay happened to look out in the hall at Harry and noticed a young woman coming down the stairs, wearing a long black dress, a traveling suit with a jacket and a long narrow skirt. She had on a little hat with a brim. "I saw her as clear as could be, and I thought she was a guest in the house. She paused on the stairs and looked real confused and shy. I called to Harry, 'I think that lady on the stairs wants to come down and leave.' Harry just looked at me and kept on talking.

"Well, I couldn't believe Harry was being so rude and said so to Danny. Then I glanced back at the group of men and the stairs and she had disappeared. I thought the poor thing was just too shy and had gone back upstairs, but five minutes later, there she was again, looking more bewildered than ever. Harry paid her no attention. Finally, after she'd come down and vanished three times, I went up to Harry and told him he was being really rude."

"Well, Gay, since you've seen her three times, I might as well tell you who she is. She isn't a guest here, Gay. She's a spirit. She lives here in the house, and Brenda and I see her all the time. We heard her many times when we were working on the house and thought it might be workmen or even the restaurant next door; their restroom is on the second floor and we thought we might be hearing vibrations from the pipes, but then we heard the noises when the restaurant was closed and knew something really strange was going on. Finally, Brenda saw her. Scared her out of her wits, but she seems harmless enough. Adds a little color to the place, don't you think?"

Everyone laughed.

Bob and Dana, who owned the B&B for several years in the mid-90s, had similar experiences. They knew about the ghost before they bought the place, but still, it was unsettling at first. One night when they were just moving in and there were no guests, they had gone to bed and were both almost asleep when they heard noises in the hall. Dana shook Bob, "I think someone is in the house."

Bob got up, grabbed a nine iron from the closet and cautiously went out into the hallway. A woman was standing there holding a small travel bag. The hair on Bob's arms bristled and he stopped. "What do you want? What are you doing here," he asked. She said nothing, not even acknowledging Bob's presence. Again in a sterner voice he demanded, "What are you doing here? Do you realize this is a private residence?" The woman melted away right in front of him. Bob stood there frozen for a few moments and then went back into the bedroom, speechless.

After that Bob and Dana saw her many times, and almost every morning. As she prepared breakfast for her guests, Dana could hear her walking about. The ghost always stayed in the hallway and on the stairs, never coming down any farther than the landing. And none of their guests ever heard or saw the woman.

Sherri and her husband, Marshall, bought the B&B in June 2000. Not long after, Sherri was in the house alone, and her television set came on. She thought that was strange but didn't think too much about it. Then, a few weeks later, she was putting towels away in a second floor closet and suddenly got the feeling someone was standing near watching her. She turned expecting to see a guest. The hall was empty. It so unnerved her that she started downstairs—and walked into a wall of icy air. She didn't go back upstairs for the rest of the day.

Months later they renovated some of the rooms, and Sherri was painting. By this time, she and her staff had had several experiences with the ghost and had even named her Mabel. Sherri was on a ladder when she heard a crackling sound, like electricity. She started to get down off the ladder to look for the source of the noise when the doorknob turned and the door opened. No one was there. Keeping her composure, she calmly asked, "Mabel, how do you like the new room?" No one answered, but the noise stopped.

On another occasion, Sherri was painting another room with a Wagner Power Painter and listening to the radio. After she'd finished the first coat, she turned the radio and the spray gun off and went down for lunch while the paint dried. When she returned, the radio was back on, tuned to a different station, and the Power Painter was spewing paint all over her nice hardwood floors. Mabel obviously didn't like the changes Sherri was making.

Sherri is a very meticulous person and went to the trouble of researching her bed and breakfast and her ghost. Apparently, the young woman was a newlywed and visiting the Pullers, the original owners of the house, on her honeymoon. On their last day in St. Augustine, her husband decided to go fishing and leave her at the house to prepare for their departure. He never returned. A squall came up, capsizing his boat, and he drowned. And the young woman died of grief soon after, having never left St. Augustine. She is here still.

Sherri would love to see Mabel reunited with her husband. On the other hand, she's fun to have around.

THE OLDEST

WOODEN SCHOOLHOUSE

You're standing at the Old City Gates looking down St. George Street at a dilapidated old wooden building—The Oldest Wooden Schoolhouse. Intrigued, you walk down the street to get a closer look. You can see the mannequins in the second-story windows. They're there to attract your attention, invite you into the place. And the heavy chain around the building just under the eaves and the anchor. What are they doing there? You find out later that they were put there in 1937 to secure the building when a hurricane threatened. The building matches the gloomy, overcast day. This is Florida—it's supposed to be sunny. So, what else do you have to do today? Go on. Buy a ticket. You know you want to see it.

You buy your ticket and enter the grounds, surprised that there are extensive gardens and other buildings, a quiet secluded compound away from the noise and crowds just on the other side of that tabby wall. You see all kinds of different vegetation, banana trees, hibiscus, birds of paradise, walks, hidden benches tucked away in cozy spots to sit on and rest, a cookhouse, an old privy, and that huge old pecan tree which must be 250 years old. And it still produces, they say.

You sit on a bench just inside the entryway and read. The house, constructed of cypress and red cedar, dates back to the eighteenth century and was originally the homestead of Juan Genoply. Wooden pegs were used to join the planks together, although some hand-wrought nails were used. Before that it was the site of an army barracks used to house off-duty soldiers stationed at the Castillo de San Marcos just across the way. Notice that the cookhouse is separated from the main building to reduce the risk of fire and the intense heat during the stifling hot summers. Can you imagine cooking over that fireplace in August? A well is nearby and a privy is farther back for a little privacy. It has a little board wall around it.

The house was probably built after 1740 when the British torched the whole town and was probably used for many purposes—a store, a tavern. But in 1788 during the Second Spanish Period it became the first co-ed school in the New World, educating both boys and girls. The classroom was on the first floor and the schoolmaster lived upstairs with his family. See, you've learned something already. You're starting to enjoy yourself in spite of the gloomy day.

You step into the yard, and suddenly you encounter the spiritual energy that fills the place. Your skin tingles as you walk throughout the grounds. The energy seems to converge around the big pecan tree. This is really strange, isn't it? Is this place haunted? You walk over to the tree and get a very clear impression of a man's dead body hanging from the tree about ten feet off the ground. At first, you're shocked but you feel no fear. You think it's strange for a man to be hanged in a schoolyard. Ah, the army barracks. Perhaps he was a prisoner of war or a soldier who had committed an act of treason. That would explain it, wouldn't it?

And do you feel like you're being watched? Oh, look up there. Is that a guard tower and is that a Spanish sentry staring at you? Can you feel his steely eyes on you? Yes, this place must really be haunted. Your skin is still tingling, and your pulse is running fast.

You go over to the cookhouse to screen yourself from the sentry in the watchtower. Strange, standing here in the doorway of the kitchen, you can't feel all that energy that surrounded you outside.

As you leave the cookhouse and walk into the main building, the energy you've been feeling in the gardens subsides a little, but it's still there. There are no ghosts down here, though. The eight or nine mannequins do nothing for you. It's interesting, though, to see the way the kids are dressed, the old map and globe, and their books. After looking around a few minutes, you step over to the stairs and look up on the second floor. There's a sign—it's closed to the public. You're disappointed, but no one else is here. Maybe the attendant will let you take a peek.

You go next door to ask if it's all right. "Sure," she says. "Go ahead. Don't stay too long though, and stay away from the windows. I don't want anyone else to think the upstairs is part of the exhibit." You thank her profusely and head back to the schoolhouse.

Once again you feel that tingling sensation as you pass into the grounds, but you ignore it and hasten into the schoolhouse and start up the stairs. When you almost reach the top, you're overcome with a feeling of nausea. You feel physically ill. What is going on? Is this a reaction to some heavy spiritual energy or an empathetic impression of someone's past illness? Did someone get sick up there? Did they die? You stumble back down the stairs to collect yourself.

After a few minutes, you're ready to try again. You just have to go up there and find out what that's all about. You take a few deep breaths and start up the stairs again, slowly. Again, you start to feel nauseous, but it's not so bad this time. You can make it. There. You're on top, and you step into the room. It's quiet up here. There's stuff all over the place. Obviously, it's used only for storage. Probably few people ever come up here.

You can feel some really serious energy up here now. Perhaps ghosts, or whatever they are, like these quiet places, and that's the reason you don't feel anything downstairs, because of all the human activity. Yes, this place is really spooky. You can feel it.

There are two mannequins, one at the front window and one at the side, but they don't seem to have any energy. No, there's something else up here. Then you notice the old frame bed on the other side of the room. Now you really start to tingle. Lying on a tattered old tick mattress is a stark white mannequin of a child, a little girl. Her painted open eyes stare, unblinking at the ceiling. In the semi-darkness of the unlit gloomy room, she looks almost alive. You expect her chest to heave as she begins breathing. She looks like a dead child lying forgotten on her bed.

Can you sense the aura in that corner of the room? It's overwhelming. Could a child have died up here? You walk over toward the bed and reach out to touch the mannequin, then pull back. You can't bring yourself to touch it. Is your presence up here bringing back some dreadful memories to a grieving spirit? You stand staring at the mannequin and then stiffen and slowly turn around.

Someone is watching you. Standing a few feet away from you along the dark west wall is a woman in her early twenties with dark brown hair tucked in a tight bun and a long, tan-colored cotton dress, very plain with a simple neckline and long sleeves, a long muslin apron around her waist. Her face is etched in sorrow. You sense at once it's a spirit. She is the young mother of a child who died in the bed! That's why you couldn't touch the mannequin.

You can feel what she's feeling. She has lost all hope. Her grief has spiraled down into deep depression. She has detached herself from all emotional ties, including those with her husband. She is little more than a zombie, and she has driven him and all others away. He leaves and stays away for long periods of time, out in the hinterlands, hunting and fishing and perhaps grieving himself for his lost wife as well as his lost child. And yet, she cannot understand why he has withdrawn from her. She does not realize that it's she who has withdrawn from him. She stares out the west window overlooking the backyard. She desperately wants her husband to return, but she also desperately wants to be alone in her grief. You feel all these things and yourself are overcome with grief. This woman is absolutely alone, trapped in this room by her sorrow and despair.

You sense that she wants to be left alone to grieve. That's why she's up here where few humans ever come. She's not mean, but she's upset that you are here. You can feel that. She tries to hide in a dark corner and is horrified when she senses that you can see her move there. She quickly moves to the opposite wall and slowly creeps along it. You can see that, too. She is trying to escape from you, but it is easy for you to follow the path of her energy. It is so strong. She does not want you to sense her grief, to feel her pain, but you can't help it. It is overwhelming. You feel so sorry for this young mother. Suddenly, you realize that you are absolutely drained, and you plod over to the stairs and down and out of the building. You want to cry for her and turn up to look at the west window. "I'm sorry," you say. "Don't despair. It's okay. You can move on. Perhaps you'll find your husband and child if you just move on," you say. Then you walk past the cookhouse and out the exit into the dreary, overcast day on St. George Street.

You think, "My, what you learn in school these days."

THE SPANISH

WASHER WOMAN

S t. George Street, running from the south end of town up to the Old Gates, has been a major thoroughfare for hundreds of years. Almost all of the older buildings on the street have been destroyed by hurricanes or fires and have long since been replaced by more modern structures. North of the Plaza, St. George Street is now entirely commercial, but it didn't used to be. For most of its four hundred years it was residential, a dirt street lined with houses where for centuries people lived, worked, played, and died. There were shops, but without exception the shopkeepers lived above or behind them, as they do even today in many places.

One of those shops that now occupy St. George Street is the Whetstone Chocolate Factory, with the Spanish Bakery behind it. The kitchen of the Spanish Bakery is actually attached to the back of Whetstone's and bakery goods are sold in a detached building behind. The entire complex is surrounded by a high wooden fence, and there are picnic tables spread around the grounds shaded by an ancient cedar tree hundreds of years old, a shady place to enjoy the delicious food and chocolates just purchased. In centuries past this place must have been someone's home, a house in front along the street, maybe a small storage building or two in the back next to a garden with corn, peppers, tomatoes, and potatoes and perhaps a few orange trees. Most certainly, there was a bench under a then much smaller cedar, a place to rest during the heat of the day. I have sat in the shade of that old cedar many times and pictured a Juan or Maria Gonzales stopping from their labors in the garden and coming over to sit beside me under that beautiful cedar to rest awhile before returning to work.

Garrett is a young actor/writer who, before he was married, lived in an apartment in a house on Charlotte Street, a block to the east of St. George. Four other young men lived in the same house, and they all worked in various jobs around the city. But they were friends and enjoyed each other's company, so three or four evenings a week after work, they would congregate with their trash at the dumpster behind the Whetstone to catch up on the day's events and plan their evening. They would often go back out on the street and up to the Mill Top for a beer and a sandwich.

One particularly hot August evening the five, as usual, straggled over toward the dumpster. Although it was just after seven o'clock, the temperature was still blistering because of the on-shore breeze, which brought high humidity. Garrett trailed about thirty yards behind the rest. The others were just entering the gate next to the Whetstone as he rounded the corner by the Mill Top. He was hurrying, and sweating a bit, to catch up.

He rushed through the gate and walked quickly toward the back of the building. As he turned the corner by the Spanish Bakery's kitchen, he was hit by a blast of cold air and froze in his tracks. He was standing almost face-to-face with a woman he did not know who was dressed in the style of the eighteenth-century inhabitants of St. Augustine. She was wearing a long, full skirt with an apron, a loose white blouse with full sleeves, and a dark bodice. Her hair was wrapped with a bandana. A stiff breeze kicked up the hem of her skirt. His first thought was that she was just one of the guides who worked across the street at the Spanish Quarter, but he quickly dismissed that thought because she didn't even acknowledge his presence and because the whole area was completely different.

The cedar tree was there but much smaller. A small orange tree grew near the back door of the bakery kitchen, and there were bushes all around covered with wet clothes, obviously drying. No benches. No trash cans. And she was standing by a large kettle hanging from a tripod over a fire, and she was stirring the contents of the kettle with a hefty pole. Garrett couldn't believe it; she was doing laundry.

He caught his breath, collected himself, and said, "Hi there." No response. She kept stirring her laundry.

Again louder and more forcefully, "Hello. How are you?" Still no response. He stood there watching her, and the realization hit him. He was watching a ghost. Was this some kind of a time warp or the intersection of two periods of time? He just stared at her. This was really weird.

Then he raced around her and the cedar tree and out the back gate to the dumpster. His friends were just standing around. "Where have you been and what are you so excited about?"

"You guys aren't going to believe this," Garrett gasped.

"What?"

"Come on. You gotta see this!"

"See what?" they demanded.

"A ghost! There's a ghost in there!"

They all dashed after Garrett as he scurried back through the gate. Seconds later all five were standing in front of the woman, astonished at what they were seeing. They were actually seeing a ghost.

"Hey, ma'am. Do you need any help?"

"Hey there."

"Hello. Hello."

"Why don't you just take this stuff to the Laundromat?"

Nothing anyone said drew any recognition or response. They were on different planes. After a few minutes, they all stood together and shouted as loudly as they could, "HELLO!" The woman stopped for a second, looked around like she might have heard something, then went back to her work. Unbelievable.

They had to tell somebody, and all five rushed off to the Mill Top to get more people to see this. When they clambered breathless up the stairs, the Mill Top went quiet, and when they related what they had seen, "There's a ghost over at the Spanish Bakery," the whole place cleared out and followed them back down the street. Less than five minutes after they had rushed out the Whetstone gate, they charged back in with a dozen others behind them.

But when they got to the end of the building, expecting to see the washerwoman, they were stunned. All they saw were picnic tables, a couple of trashcans, and the big, old cedar tree. There was no woman. There was no fire and no tripod. There were no bushes and no laundry drying. There was no orange tree. Garrett felt the ground where the fire had been and it wasn't even warm.

But that isn't the end of the story. Garrett, who was a tour guide for Tour St. Augustine's "A Ghostly Experience," told his boss, Sandy, about it, and Sandy asked permission from Marge and Dewey of the Spanish Bakery to use the story on her tour. Marge and Dewey said yes. The day after Halloween, Cindy, one of the tour guides, called Marge and thanked her.

"Thanks for what?" asked Marge.

"For the visual effects, the soap suds."

"What are you talking about?"

"Well, you know on the tour, we tell the story of the lady doing her laundry and all, and, then, you know, you had all those soap suds in the cedar tree. It was a nice effect. Pretty cool."

In a somewhat shaken voice Marge replied, "Cindy, we didn't put any soap suds in that tree. That's ridiculous."

There was silence for a minute. "Then . . . who?" Cindy's voice trailed off.

Gene, the baker for the Spanish Bakery, comes to work very early to start baking for the day. With a little coaxing he admits that he has never actually seen a ghost, but he does say that he hears noises all that time, people walking around, the sound of a hoe tilling the earth. He has also seen his baking equipment moving around.

Marge, Dewey, Gene, and their crew all accept that there is at least one ghost on the premises and have named her Julie. She doesn't bother them very much. In fact, Gene often wonders if he might get her to do some baking so he wouldn't have to come in quite so early.

CASA DE SUEÑOS

Kathleen Hurley, the present owner of the Casa de Sueños, chatted as she led me through her elegant bed and breakfast on the corner of Saragossa and Cordova Streets. "The house was built in 1904 as a story-and-a-half residence and was transformed in 1920 to a lovely Mediterranean-style two-story by a cigar maker from Spain. During the mid-1900s, it served as a funeral home owned by Mr. Garcia. Bill McGrath, who lived nearby on Saragossa, was the funeral director."

Kathleen doesn't exactly scoff at the idea of ghosts and hauntings. "I do believe there could be spirits here, but I'm not over the top trying to create them." She believes the ghost business in St. Augustine has gotten a bit out of hand. Once when she was doing some construction work on the front of the house, she overheard a tour guide explain that the freshly dug earth was the grave of someone who had died in the place. And trolley and carriage drivers often refer to the B&B as "the old haunted funeral home" as they pass by. Kathleen just smiles and shakes her head.

She prefers to believe in coincidences, because there are a lot of things she can't explain. In 1956 when she was a little girl she and her family came to visit St. Augustine. She remembers visiting the Oldest Wooden Schoolhouse and walking all over town. She surely walked past the bed and breakfast, which was a funeral home at the time, although she doesn't remember specifically. She even has a postcard, which is now mounted in a collage on her wall, that she and her sister sent to their aunt from St. Augustine. That was her only visit. She vaguely remembers that the trip was boring.

Then in 2001, after thirty-two years in the corporate world with monthly trips to New York and almost constant global travel, she decided she'd had enough. Business travel was getting too stressful and demanding. Her dream had always been to open a bed and breakfast, so she retired from corporate life and went looking for her dream B&B. At first she was interested in Savannah, but friends told her she should look in the charming little city of St. Augustine, too. Her first thought was of the boring trip she'd taken as a child, but she decided to go to St. Augustine and have a look. It was so close to Savannah.

The owners of the Casa de Sueños showed her the B&B, drove her around St. Augustine, and even introduced her to Bill McGrath, the former funeral director. He regaled her with stories about the house and about St. Augustine. She liked the house, St. Augustine, and the elderly Irish gentleman who reminded her of her father, but she was ready to see some other places. During the next few weeks and months, Kathleen looked at eighteen bed and breakfasts between St. Augustine and Wilmington, North Carolina. In the end the Casa de Sueños drew her back to St. Augustine like a magnet, and she bought it in July 2001. And the day she closed on the B&B, Mr. McGrath died peacefully in his own bed in his beach house nearby. Nothing traumatic, but Kathleen had the serene feeling that he was turning the place over to her. A coincidence?

"As I said, when I was working I went to New York a lot, often several times a month. And after September 11, all these friends from New York called, 'How did you know to get out of here when you did? How did you know?' Of course, I didn't, but perhaps that was another coincidence for me," Kathleen said.

Fifteen or so years ago while she was living in North Carolina, she bought a mirror. When she was moving into the Casa de Sueños, she stood in her dining room surrounded by boxes. As she opened and unpacked each box, she came across the mirror she had purchased so long ago. She took it out of the box, unwrapped it, and held it up to look for cracks or other damage. She was astonished to see that the mirror matched the shape and design of the dining room windows exactly. Yes, Kathleen Hurley believes in coincidences.

She does admit, reluctantly, that she has at least one ghost in the Casa de Sueños, however—Randolph. That's the name she and her staff, Monica and Carol Ann, have given him. When Kathleen first moved in, she was alone in her office one evening amid stacks of boxes, sorting things and putting them away. Suddenly, all the stuff in one of the boxes just seemed to jump out and land on the floor. The box was sitting on the floor and didn't fall over. The things inside just jumped out. Needless to say, Kathleen was startled. Several days later, a candle did the same thing, jumping out of the box it was in.

Whenever the staff can't find a key or something weird happens, they speak to Randolph about it, "Come on, Randolph, give it back," and it shows up. One recent Sunday morning, Carol Ann and

Kathleen were sitting in the sunroom. There wasn't another soul in the house. All of a sudden, they heard a loud kaboom! as if a large heavy object had been dropped on the floor—a coffin perhaps? "What the heck was that?" Kathleen asked.

Carol answered, "I don't know, but we don't have any ghosts, right?"

They both laughed. No. No ghosts, only coincidences.

SCARLETT

O'HARA'S

*A*my had just turned off the lights, set the alarm, and locked up at Scarlett O'Hara's. She hurried down the steps and headed for home, but before she had even cleared the end of the building, the alarm went off inside. "Oh no, not again," she thought and turned back toward the building. Before she even got to the door, the police arrived. Amy unlocked the front door, and Brandon and his partner rushed in. Brandon began checking the first floor and his partner bounded upstairs. Moments later he rushed back down again. "Brandon, you're not going to believe this. You know that barber's chair next to the window? It was facing the window when I got to the top of the stairs. As I came nearer, the chair turned all the way around, and I swear to God it moved just like someone was getting out of it. Spooky!"

Both officers went back upstairs, since Brandon's partner

was not too keen on going up again by himself. When he went into the restroom, someone put a hand on his shoulder. It wasn't Brandon. At that point the policemen had had enough and went back downstairs.

Brandon laughed. This was not the first time he had responded to an alarm at Scarlett O'Hara's. It is a spooky place, although the two known ghosts who live there are perfectly harmless. The building was originally a house and has a long history.

A Mr. Colee built it as a home for his fiancée in 1879. Before the house was even finished, she jilted him and ran off to marry a soldier stationed at the fort. Mr. Colee was understandably upset. Shortly after, however, he did marry another woman. Soon after he did, his wife found him dead, drowned in his own bathtub. At first, everyone thought he had killed himself, but later evidence indicated that he might have had some help—and probably from his ex-fiancée's new husband.

Mr. Colee's family lived in the house until the mid-1950s, when it was closed and boarded up until 1979. Then Kevin Finch purchased it. He attached the house next to it, made some major renovations, and opened Scarlett O'Hara's. In 1998 John Arbezani, the present owner, bought the restaurant. Situated across from Flagler College, it is a lively watering hole—live music nightly, dining both inside and on the porch during good weather, an outside oyster bar, and a martini bar on the second floor.

Mr. Colee likes the second-floor martini bar, appropriately named the Ghost Bar, and more particularly the men's room. On many occasions, an excited man has rushed out of the restroom, unnerved by a hand on his shoulder or someone's hot breath on the back of his neck while he's standing at the urinal. The old barber's chair has been removed, but the other chairs still turn and move around.

For atmosphere, Rick, the general manager, has placed lots of candles around the upstairs bar. One day Captain Tom, who has long been a bartender at Scarlett's, went upstairs to open things up, and as he reached the top of the staircase, the dozen or so candles all simultaneously lit. Mr. Colee likes the candles. Captain Tom just shook his head and went about his business.

Mr. Colee also likes to play with the heating and air conditioning system. When it's hot out, he likes to turn the heat on, and when it's cold he prefers the air conditioning. And he loves television. He's a surfer. Patrons get exasperated with him at times. Can you imagine watching the last two minutes of a tied NFL football game and have the channel switched to the Food Network? Mr. Colee does it all the time.

Mr. Colee's picture is bolted to the brick chimney on the west wall upstairs. He was a quite handsome fellow. For many years the picture moved almost daily from one wall to another to a door and back again. Captain Tom related that once they bolted the picture to a door. The following day when they opened, it was on a wall. Finally, someone suggested that they try hanging it on the brick chimney. Mr. Colee seems to like it there. The picture hasn't moved since.

Another ghost inhabits Scarlett O'Hara's. He hangs around downstairs in the main bar, usually on the north side of the building. No one has identified him, but Captain Tom sees him all the time. "One day I was standing at the end of the bar reading my paper, and someone walked past me. He went to the very end of the bar and pulled out a stool. I looked up to greet him—and he disappeared. Talk about getting nervous. That was the first time anyone had seen him in the daytime. Usually after closing, someone will see him walk through toward the far end, and when we go down to check no one is there."

I visited Scarlett O'Hara's around Christmas time and chuck-led to see Christmas stockings for each employee hanging around the fireplace. Mr. Colee's stocking was among them, but I didn't see one for the unidentified stranger. So I asked Captain Tom about the omission. He just shrugged. Since they didn't know who he was, they saw no need for a stocking. The stranger seems not to have taken any offense.

THE MINORCANS

*I*n 1768 during the period of British rule, Dr. Andrew Turnbull established a colony at New Smyrna and recruited 1,400 Minorcan, Greek, and Italian laborers to raise indigo and food crops. Conditions in New Smyrna were deplorable and made worse by the toxic process used with the indigo. Finally, after many complaints of cruel treatment to Governor Tonyn in St. Augustine, the remaining group of six hundred Minorcans, as the whole group was called, was released from their indentures and, led by Francisco Pellicer and their priest, Father Pedro Camps, marched north to settle in St. Augustine.

Most of the families settled in the northwest quarter of the city, an area that became known as the Minorcan Quarter. By 1786 when the Spanish were again in control of Florida and St. Augustine, the Minorcans numbered 469 (they had been reduced to 469 from the original 600 who marched up to St. Augustine from New Smyrna), more than half the population of the city, and had become an integral force in the town.

One of the priests under Father Camps established what was probably the first free public school in North America. It was initially located at the corner of Bridge and Saint George Streets across from the Old St. Augustine Village. White boys were required to attend, blacks could if they wished, and all lessons were in Spanish. The Minorcan boys were punished for speaking their own dialect.

But the Minorcans continued to prosper, often providing fresh vegetables from their gardens and fish from the sea to other townspeople who had little else to eat. Over the centuries they became the glue that held St. Augustine together and today remain a significant influence in the life of the Ancient City.

The Minorcans have a secret to their longevity—family. The family holds them together. Family is taken into account in every decision a Minorcan makes. And family includes both living and dead. Marie's family is a good example.

Marie lives on one of the streets in the Minorcan Quarter in a single-story house her great-grandfather built in 1888. He had purchased five lots from his brother-in-law and built his first home on the middle lot. Other family members had houses on the same street. In fact, in the beginning, only Minorcans lived on the street. That first house was a small Victorian home with a separate kitchen behind. When her grandfather grew up and married, he, his bride, his parents, and his aunt all lived in the same house. Later her grandfather built a large two-story home next door. The little house was rented to other family members.

In 1940 Marie's parents married and were given the little house as a wedding present. Marie, her two brothers, and two sisters were all born and grew up in this home. Marie has fond memories of growing up surrounded by grandparents, aunts and uncles, and many, many cousins, all Minorcans, all living on the same street.

Their street was a family street, and life during Marie's childhood centered on the screened front porch. No one had television in those days and so people spent their evenings sitting out talking and visiting neighbors, while the kids raced around in the street. "During much of the year, we lived on the porch. We ate supper on the porch. After our baths, we had our ice cream on the porch. I can remember so many evenings, falling asleep out there and Daddy carrying me back in the house to bed," Marie sighs nostalgically.

"And then there was the beach," she continues. "On hot summer afternoons Daddy and Mother would pack us all in the car. Our aunts and uncles up the street and Daddy's two cousins around the corner would do the same, and we'd all head out to the beach, just dozens of us. The men would fish and the kids would swim and tear around, while our mothers watched us with eyes in the backs of their heads. If the men caught any fish, we'd eat them. Otherwise, Mother would always have hot dogs to roast. She never counted on the men catching anything. Then at dark we'd pack up and head home, and we always ended our evenings on the porch."

There was also the cemetery. Almost every Saturday of their young lives, Papa, Marie's grandfather, would take the kids to the family cemetery. He was the caretaker then, a job Marie has since inherited. They'd help him clean the debris off the graves and put out flowers. Then they were allowed to run around and look at things. Seeing all the graves of family members when she was little really helped her to understand the importance of family.

"When I first moved into the little house, I had some bad feelings about the living room. That's where my great-grandmother, Mama Kay, died and where her wake was held. She died before I was born, so I never knew her, but Daddy said she was a pretty grumpy old woman and didn't like him at all. Well, I just didn't feel comfortable in that living room. Finally, one Saturday, when I went out to the cemetery to take care of the graves, I took an extra big bunch of flowers with me and put them on Mama Kay's grave. Then I told her that I knew she didn't like Daddy and she probably wouldn't have liked me if she'd known me, but as long as I was alive I would see that she had fresh flowers on her grave and, even though I never knew her, I loved her because she was my great-grandmother. Well, you know, after that I never had any more of those bad feelings in the living room. In fact, it's my favorite room in the house now."

At the end of their lives, Marie's mother had to be moved to a nursing home, but her father still lived next door. Marie's children were grown and she had few obligations so she moved into the little house to look after him. "Daddy got lonesome," she recalls, "so every night after work I'd go over and have supper with him. Now, I believe in spirits, but I didn't think he did. However, one night I asked him, 'Daddy, you've lived all your life in these two houses. Are you going to tell me you've never seen any spirits?' He sighed and said that of course he did. 'I've seen 'em, Marie, but they are family. Always remember they're in your family and they're not going to harm you.'

"So, after he died I had some really strange things here in the little house and I said, 'Dad, I don't mind taking care of the family houses. I don't even mind taking care of the family cemetery, but did you have to send all the family spirits over here? Couldn't some of them stay next door?' Well, some of them have gone back. I'm just as happy with the spirits of my ancestors as I am with my living family members, and they like it here too, I think."

Her first experience in the little house was when her mother had gone to the nursing home. She was working and then going to spend time with her. Marie came home late one evening and stopped by her son Darrell's house—he lived in the house behind her. She looked over at her house and saw that the kitchen light was on. "What's going on over there?" she asked.

He said, "Well, don't you always leave a light on?"

"Yes," she said, "but not in the kitchen. I leave the living room light on."

"Oh, for God's sake, it's your imagination. Go home." She went home. The kitchen light was on, and the living room light was turned off.

And not long after she had another strange incident. Her son and his wife put their bicycles on Marie's front porch and locked the door, not thinking anything about it. Later that night someone slit the screen and stole the bikes. After that she started leaving the porch light on all night.

One morning soon after she started leaving the porch light on, she got up and the bathroom light was on. She could see the bathroom from the bedroom and knew she couldn't have turned on the light. She went on to work and that evening came home and said, "Okay, let's have a talk about this. You don't turn lights on. You leave the lights alone." Later, she went out, turned on the porch light, and went to bed.

The next morning, the bathroom light was off but so was the porch light. That night she had another little talk with her spirits. "Okay, let's discuss this one more time. If I turn lights on, you leave them on. If I turn lights off, you leave them off. I don't want to see you or hear you. You can stay as long as you want, but you have to follow the rules." She's had no more trouble with lights, except for one time.

She and a friend were taking a Florida history class in Jacksonville and didn't get home until about nine-thirty. Darrell was standing in the drive waiting for her.

"What's going on?" she asked.

He said that he had been on her back porch using the washer and dryer when he heard footsteps in the house. He ran home and from his place could see what looked like a flashlight moving around the house. He called the police. They responded immediately but didn't find anything. Marie called them again.

"Ma'am, we've already been out there."

"I don't care," she said. "I'm not going in that house without a cop with me. Just send somebody."

The officer they sent was the same one who'd come earlier. They entered and walked all through the house. Nothing was disturbed.

"Darrell, are you sure it wasn't a spirit walking around in here?"

He gave her his usual, "Oh, for God's sake. It's your imagination, Mother."

The policeman was unnerved. "Lady, please don't talk like that. I just came from a house on Aviles Street and what happened there no human being did. If you keep this up, I'm not going to sleep all night."

Marie just smiled, "Well, spirits are in there, but I usually don't hear them."

A couple of years later Marie was sitting on the side porch, now a TV room, talking on the phone. She happened to look into the dining room, and a man was seated there. He was just watching her. He was wearing a brown suit and didn't look like anyone she'd seen in any family pictures. She didn't want to scream because she was talking on the phone, so she just closed her eyes and took a breath. When she opened her eyes, he was gone.

Then about six months later, she was again watching television. She glanced over toward the dining room, and standing in the doorway was a little girl about ten years old. She had a big bow on top of her hair and long curls. The girl was wearing a light-colored dress and, like the man earlier, was staring at her. Marie didn't say anything, just looked back at the TV, then back at the girl. She was gone.

The strangest thing happened about two years ago. Marie got out of the shower one day and there was a funny face drawn in the condensation on the mirror. Only it wasn't done with someone's finger, because when the condensation cleared, the funny face was gone. She didn't think anything about it though. She decided perhaps one of the grandchildren had done it.

But a couple of nights later, she climbed out of the shower again and the words PEACE OUT were written on the mirror. That really unnerved her. She knew her father had said the spirits in her house were family and they wouldn't hurt her, but she thought this was really weird. Darrell came over and they cleaned off the mirror but could still see the words PEACE OUT. They even steamed the room up again and wrote PEACE OUT on the mirror. When the steam cleared they could see the letters they had written and the original PEACE OUT. However, when they cleaned the mirror, their writing was gone—the other words, the original PEACE OUT, were still there. Marie spent the next few nights at Darrell's house.

A short time later a parapsychologist from Gainesville came over and talked with Marie for a long time. She couldn't understand why these things were happening to her, because she'd never been particularly sensitive in the past. He explained that spirits sometimes pass through, but she didn't think that was it. Marie thought that these were family members, related to the house. The parapsychologist told her that she could build a force field and keep them out. But Marie just couldn't do that to her own family. She decided to let them stay and have their fun.

A couple of years ago, the house across the street from Marie's caught fire. She heard the fire trucks and ran over to help the elderly couple that lived there. Not one other neighbor appeared, and it haunted Marie for several days. She decided then that she would do something about it. Her street was built for families, for people to know and help each other. She realized that she was the last Minorcan left on the street.

Now once or twice a year she gets her neighbors together and tells them stories about the neighborhood. Most of the people have learned their neighbor's names, and they have heard all the tales about Marie's relatives, including the spirits who live on the street. She won't let them forget that Minorcans built this street and this neighborhood and that family is everything.

DOGS AND

DEMONS

*J*oe had done two tours in Vietnam as a Marine infantryman. He had been wounded three times and was highly decorated. After Vietnam, he had returned to the States and had started working for the Sheriff's Department, where he quickly earned a reputation for fearlessness and professionalism. Eventually, he became head of the Canine Corps. Joe was a no-nonsense, serious-minded officer, not easily rattled and not given to outbursts of emotion.

Joe always had a lot of dogs around his house. Officers and their dogs are inseparable, but there is always turnover, officers and dogs retiring, new ones coming into the department. So Joe, as head of the department, usually had several dogs at home.

Police dogs have a reputation for being aggressive and dangerous, but most aren't. They are extremely intelligent and highly trained for a variety of nonviolent tasks, and Joe often walked the dogs around town in the evening to give them a little exercise, the dogs being accustomed to strenuous activity.

One crisp winter evening Joe took Spike, a German Shepherd, for a long walk. It was late, and few cars were on the streets. They saw no one else walking. Nothing stirred. There was not a breath of a breeze. Stars blazed in the steel-blue night sky. Up by the Castillo, Joe unsnapped Spike's leash. He was a very bright dog and so well-trained to both voice and hand signals, Joe saw no problem in letting the dog run free for a bit. They continued their walk, Joe putting Spike at heel near the main streets, although there was no need, so few cars were about.

As they approached the cemetery, the canopy of the surrounding oaks closed in, blotting out the starlight and much of the light from neighboring homes and stores and the street lamps on adjacent streets. Spike was perhaps ten yards in front of Joe when he stopped and started yelping. Joe quickly commanded him to stay and hurried up to the dog. Spike continued yelping and hopping around. The hair on his back was standing straight up. Joe knelt down and talked softly to the dog trying to calm him down, but it was no use. Spike was very upset. Joe stood, started walking away, and commanded Spike to heel. Disregarding all of his training, Spike barked twice and sped in the opposite direction toward the cemetery. Joe ran after him. He could no longer see Spike, but, as he ran up the sidewalk, he could hear a commotion. Spike was snarling and barking at something, obviously aggravated.

When Joe reached the cemetery, Spike had entered and was near a grave snapping and barking at something. Joe could not see what it was. He climbed over the fence and had almost reached Spike when he looked up and was stunned to see before him a sight that filled him with terror. Rising out of the earth was a glowing, bluish-green funnel of mist that reminded him of a tornado. The top of this mass looked vaguely like a human upper torso, but the face was indescribable, demonic with eyes that penetrated like lasers. It was looking at Spike, still prancing and bounding around the grave, obviously disturbed by the dog's presence. As Joe approached, the creature's evil gaze turned toward him. Spike raced away, but Joe was frozen to the spot, petrified by the demon's icy, malevolent glare. Joe absolutely could not move. For ten seconds that seemed like ten centuries, the beast stared at him as if it knew Joe should-n't have been there and shouldn't have seen it. Then it imploded back into the earth of the grave.

Joe stood motionless for a few moments, then turned and raced for home, vaulting the fence and not stopping until he had reached his door. Spike was sitting on the porch quivering and whining.

Some time later, Joe's wife, Karen, and her sister, Susan, came home and found Joe sitting hysterical at the kitchen table. Spike was pacing around the kitchen, still quivering and whining. Joe's face was ashen and he was sobbing, speechless. "We thought he'd killed someone," Karen later said. She put her arms around him to comfort him while Susan got Joe a drink. Finally, after nearly thirty minutes, he was able to relate what had happened.

Spike was useless after this encounter and had to retire. He lives with Joe. Joe took the rest of the week off and eventually got back to work. He still takes dogs home with him and walks them but never goes near the cemetery—any cemetery—and Spike won't go out after dark.

OLD CITY HOUSE

*L*et me introduce myself. My name is Crumpet, and I own the magnificent Old City House just south of the Casa Monica on Cordova Street. I am a dog, but not just any dog—I'm a Jack Russell. Officially, James and Ilse are on the deed for the place, but we're family and partners, so I figure I'm just as much an owner as they are. From the beginning of our association we have done everything together. I have gone on planes with them, into restaurants, to parties, on long motor trips. We have always been inseparable. So, I think they would agree that I'm as much a partner as either of them.

When we bought the place, I was excited. I mean, think of it. The house was built in 1873 as a stable and carriage house. A man named Holmes Ammidown built it and a mansion where the parking lot is now over on Saint George Street. And, as we found out later, there was a Spanish guardhouse on the site long before Mr. Ammidown's stable. The mansion burned down about seventy-five years ago, but the stable continued in use for a time serving the Flagler hotels. Then it became a series of residences, shops, an attorney's office, and, finally, about ten years ago, a bed and breakfast and renowned restaurant. Can you just imagine the wonderful smells that someone like me could pick up in a place like this? I just knew it was going to be heaven.

Well, from the very first time we entered the place, I was, shall I say, uncomfortable, especially in the hallway and the dining room. I didn't want to say anything, but I could tell immediately that we had a ghost on the premises. Ilse and James could tell that I was not happy because of my somewhat peculiar behavior. As soon as we came in I would go right to the door and scratch to be let out, things like that, you know. Because of their limited means of human communication, I couldn't tell them about the ghost. I suppose they attributed my behavior to some sort of scent that I didn't like. They had no idea there was a ghost. He wasn't mean or anything. He was just there and I was just uncomfortable. That's all.

I decided to put my feelings aside and get on with it. After all, this place was a dream for both Ilse and James. Ilse, who was born in South Africa and was working in the pharmaceutical industry, fantasized about moving to St. Augustine and owning a small inn. Born in England, James came to America as a child and was an engineer in Boston. He got tired of the corporate life and dreamed also of owning an inn. He moved to St. Augustine and, shortly after, met Ilse in an English pub. Their meeting was no accident, I can tell you. Six months later they married and bought the Old City House, or I should say, we bought it.

It took us nine months to renovate it the way we wanted. We had decided to recapture the building's old Mediterranean feel, to fit the ambiance of the town, and to make it a more romantic place. Personally, I think we've down an incredible job of it.

Six months after we finished the renovation and opened our

doors for business, we had a "cheese and wine," as James calls it, for the guests in the Inn on the upper deck. We had a full house, fourteen guests, and it was a Saturday night. Normally, I wasn't allowed up there, but that hallway was so unnerving, I sneaked up the stairs and sat behind a potted palm. The guests were all talking and having a good time. Eventually, the subject of ghosts came up, as it often does here in St. Augustine. They had all been on a ghost tour the night before. In fact, many of them had noted that one of the guests, a woman named Kim, had several times pre-empted the ghost tour guide. She seemed to be quite authoritative, especially about ghosts. Apparently, she had actually seen some ghosts on the tour. Anyway, someone asked her, "What exactly was going on last night when we were on the tour? I mean, you seemed to know more than the guide."

Kim was a very nice lady. She answered, "Well, I suppose I should have said something, but, you see, I'm a medium, and there were all sorts of things going on that I knew the guide was unaware of. That's why I sounded so . . . "

You can imagine—the cheese and wine got pretty interesting. Kim soon had the whole crowd transfixed with her experiences. James, I suppose, was thinking about the age of the building, although still not knowing anything about the ghost. He asked her, "This building is quite old. Do you think we have any ghosts here?"

"As a matter of fact," she answered, "you do have a ghost here. He was a Spanish soldier here about three hundred years ago. This was his guard post. He was killed by an accidental discharge of his own musket. I don't think he realizes he's dead, and he continues to patrol up and down the area of your hallway downstairs. By the way, having the ghost of a Spanish sentry on your property is a good omen, you know."

I could have told him that!

"Ah, so that's why Crumpet is so nervous down there," he replied.

"Exactly, that's very typical of animals. They sense things like that."

Well, Kim came back several times and even contacted and saw the ghost. She did a charcoal drawing of him and gave it to Ilse and James. If you ask them, they might let you see it.

A few months after this, we walked over to Peterson's Bakery around the corner on King Street to get breakfast breads. We went in and introduced ourselves as the new owners of the Old City House and got to talking with the owner of the bakery. She has been involved with many of the archeological digs in town and was quite knowledgeable. And, did you know, whenever there is any construction here in St. Augustine, we must first conduct an archeological dig? I think that is very admirable, don't you?

Anyway, she started telling us what an unusual and interesting piece of property we had. She went on to say that in the 1700s the Rosario defense line, the city wall, came right down Cordova Street through where our Inn now stands. That would mean just about right past the hallway. When the previous owner had remodeled, they had found a lot of coquina block from the old sentry station and had used it on the front façade of the inn. Well, Ilse, James, and I were just astounded. It finally all fit together.

Not so long ago there was a huge ghost hunt, I guess you'd call it, here in St. Augustine. Several paranormal research groups took part with cameras, electromagnetic meters, and tape recorders. They came to the inn and found all kinds of activity. They picked up distinct forms all up and down the hallway. And James, he was so funny. He was taking pictures of his own. He would stand in one place and take several pictures in succession. When he had them developed, there were several orbs in the pictures, only they moved from one spot to another in each of the pictures. It was certainly exciting having all those strange people around.

And from the very first, guests have noticed tapping in the front area of the inn, especially in the Lightner Room and down in the Augustin Room. A lot of people have heard about it. Of course, I knew what it was right away, but James had no idea and was always trying to figure it out. He thought it couldn't be the pipes because they were all PVC, and it couldn't be the electrostatic lighter on the hot water heater, because it makes more of a clicking sound, and it isn't very loud anyway. And, obviously, it wasn't the washing machine, not at three in the morning.

Once in the first year, James and I were hanging curtains in the Augustin Room— he was on a ladder, and I was supervising. We heard this very distinct, loud knock. Well, I knew exactly who it was and where it was coming from, but James couldn't figure it out. The knocking went on for perhaps ten or fifteen seconds, so James got down off the ladder and started walking around trying to determine where the noise was coming from. He checked the door, the walls, the floor, each of the corners. He had no idea. If only he had a better command of animal languages, I could have told him.

Recently up in the Lightner Room the guests said they were awakened by what they thought was a knock on the door. They got up and went to the door. There was no one there. We have these strange little things happening here all the time.

I don't get down to the inn as much now as I used to. Last year we had these precious babies, twin girls. Well, Ilse had them, actually. Now with the girls at home I have other duties that I have to attend to, but I still enjoy going to the inn occasionally, even if I get a little scared at times. The sentry is a good ghost, very professional. But what I like best are the smells. Can you imagine the aroma of three-hundred-year-old Spanish chorizo? Delicious!

THE PUMPKIN

CHURCH

*T*he Reverend John Jerry, a Methodist circuit rider, brought Methodism to St. Augustine when it was transferred from Spain to the United States in 1821, under General Andrew Jackson. Thirty-four ministers have served this Methodist flock since then. The first Methodist church in St. Augustine was a fourteen-by-thirty-one-foot structure known as the Bethel Church.

The present First Methodist Church, affectionately known as the Pumpkin Church because of its orange color, was built in 1911. It has undergone many, many changes. Several additions and property purchases have expanded it to its present size, and to say that it is quaint now would be an understatement. There are nooks and crannies, closed-off rooms, boarded up doors, crawl spaces, and extraneous stairs all over. Nanette, the caretaker, related that there is a sealed room in the top of the bell tower, which she went into once. It had not been occupied for years,

but, when she entered it, it contained a chair, dresser, and mirror—
and it was as neat, tidy, and dust free as her own home.

Nanette also has had some ghostly experiences in the church.
One evening she was working, vacuuming down the center aisle,
but she was tired. The past week of vacation bible school had been
a long one, and, after being with dozens of children every day for
the last five days, she was ready to go home. It was late. It was very,
very hot. And it was about to rain. She had cleaned the fellowship
hall, the kitchen, and the offices upstairs, and now she was almost
finished.

As she worked the thunder outside got closer and more frequent. It's about to rain, she thought. Better get that trash to the
dumpster. She went to the side door, picked up the bags of trash she
had left there, and headed outside. But she was too late. The rain
pelted her as she ran to the dumpster across the parking lot. By the
time she returned she was soaked, so she went to the kitchen to get
a towel.

As she entered the darkened room, a clap of thunder boomed
very near the church, rattling the windows, and just at that moment
a rat ran across the top of the freezer less than three feet away.
Nanette screamed. Her heart leapt into her throat. She stood there
a moment to calm down. Then, she backed out of the kitchen. No
need to go in there anymore. She'd already cleaned the place, and
she really didn't need that towel.

Back in the sanctuary she continued sweeping the aisles. Night
was descending, and the rain continued unabated. She was working
down the center aisle towards the altar when, suddenly, a spot light
in the balcony came on. "I couldn't see up in the balcony, of course,
because the light blinded me, and I didn't hear anything. Well, I
couldn't hear anything because of the rain outside, but I didn't really think anything about the light. I just thought it was a short or

something. I wasn't going to go up into that dark balcony to check it, though, so I called my husband. He said he couldn't come for a while, and I went back to vacuuming."

On the street-side of the church toward the back is a small sound booth that contains the control equipment for the sound system. The booth juts out a little from the wall and has a window in front so the soundman can see the front of the church. As Nanette worked her way back up, she started hearing this tinkling sound, like tiny bells, barely audible. And then, boom! Music blasted over the surround-sound system, enveloping her like a spider web, completely shattering her nerves. She jumped in panic and raced back down the center aisle toward the front of the church, her heart beating wildly. When she got in front of the altar, she stopped not knowing what else to do. She took a few deep breaths to calm herself, and then said a little prayer.

"When I first started working at the church, Reverend McQueen came in while I was cleaning and sat down in a pew to talk. He said, 'I just wanted to let you know that there are some people in the church who believe there are ghosts here.'

"He was, like, warning me, I guess. Well, I didn't want to see a ghost. I didn't want to hear a ghost. I didn't want to talk about a ghost or even think about one."

Outside the storm raged. Inside the spotlight still glared down on her and the music pounded in her ears. Her nerves were raw. What if the electricity went off? Again, she panicked. Jumping up to the level of the altar, she rummaged through the lecterns on both sides, looking for a flashlight. Nothing. Finally, she found a candle and some matches. Well, that, at least, was something.

"I'm thinking, this is too weird and to go farther back into the darkness in the back—I don't think so, not with this dinky candle. I called my husband again. He laughed a little but said he'd come as soon as he could—only he couldn't for about another hour. My heart sank."

"Well, I thought maybe I can at least go back and do the men's restroom, and I tried, but as I walked toward the darkness at the back of the church, I started thinking, the rat, the light, the music. Nah, I'm out of here."

She called her husband to let him know she'd be across the street at the Gigglin' Gator, and she squished her way across King Street. Her husband found her at the bar finishing off a margarita.

"There was another time when I was vacuuming down near the altar late one afternoon. I was just working along, not thinking, just pushing my vacuum cleaner back and forth when suddenly there was this bam, bam, bam at the main front door. It was like someone was smashing it using a telephone pole for a battering ram. I froze. I could not move. Okay, it was daylight and not really a problem, but after I composed myself, I went outside and walked around the church. And, of course, there was nothing there anywhere which could have made that sound.

And then, there was an incident with Susan, the secretary, who also coordinates weddings. She had just finished up with a wedding. The wedding party had left and she was straightening up. Her husband and daughter were waiting for her in the fellowship hall. As they were standing there, they both saw her through the kitchen's pass-through window walking across the kitchen. Just then, she came into the hall from the sanctuary behind them. They were shocked. Who had they seen?

"It's not that I don't believe in ghosts," Paul, the youth minister, says. "It's just that I don't choose to dabble in that. But, once during a 'lockup' when the youth group spent the night in the church, the kids saw a woman in a polka dot dress, back behind the choir area. There's a room back there that gets scary after dark. A very steep stairway goes up and once up there, you have to stoop to go under a rounded doorway. To the right is a storage room and to the left and above is a trap door. Very spooky at night. Anyway, some of the kids saw a woman in a polka dot dress.

"Well, some of them got pretty scared, so I brought them all into the sanctuary and we talked about it. I just told them, 'You know, we have lots of weddings and baptisms here, but we have just as many funerals. It's a part of life as much as a baptism.' I pointed to right in front of the altar and said, 'Just last week on this very spot there was the body of someone who had been alive the week before. Death is part of life.' I told them not to scare them, but just to explain."

My friend, Kristine, is a member of First Methodist and believes in ghosts. She is comforted by the fact that some like it there so much they don't want to leave. "That says a lot for this church. It's a wonderful place to worship."

I agree with her.

O.C. WHITE'S

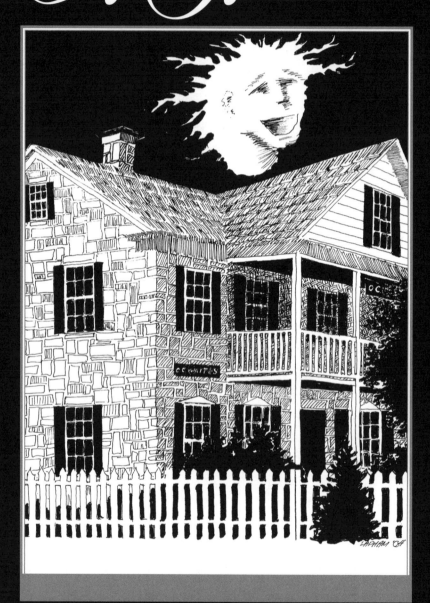

*D*ave got out of his car and approached the burned-out hulk of his restaurant with trepidation. This place had been his dream, and he was still suffering the pain of the loss. It was late, after midnight. A chilly, fog-laden breeze blew in from the ocean, which made the evening that much gloomier. He had meant to come earlier, but there was so much to do—insurance forms, police reports—and he had just run out of time. He was tired and feeling not a little overwhelmed, but he had to get this done.

The fire had left the first floor windows intact, but the heat had blasted out the second- and third-floor windows. With the first floor closed up he hadn't been worried about vandalism and had planned to leave the upper windows open to help air the place out. He was already thinking about rebuilding and about how soon he could reopen. The night before, however, vandals had scaled the walls to the second-floor balcony and gotten into the place, not that there was much to vandalize. The thieves had stolen the stereo, which hadn't been burned, and had smashed the cigarette machines to steal all the cigarettes. Now, he was forced to board up at least the second-story windows. He'd had plywood delivered earlier and was here to finish off the last of his "to do" list for the day.

Dave unlocked the front door and flashed his light around. There was an opening in the second floor over the bar and entry way with a banister around it, and he could see all the charred wood upstairs. My poor restaurant, he thought. Then he fastened on his carpenter's belt, grabbed the first piece of plywood and stumbled through the darkness to the stairs, following the beam of his flash-light. He went to the first window at the top of the stairs on the east side of the building and got to work. He first hoisted the plywood up to fit the window as best he could, then began nailing. It was hard work he wasn't really up for, so he was concentrating.

Suddenly, a woman started screaming at him from behind. Startled, he jumped, dropped his hammer, and spun around. He couldn't see her or understand what she was saying, but the sound was coming from the opening in the floor. It wasn't coming from below either. It was coming from mid-air. Dave didn't believe in ghosts, but this incident totally unnerved him. He left his hammer and quickly retraced his steps downstairs and out of the building.

*   *   *   *

In 1791 Don Miguel Ysnardy constructed a Spanish Colonial–style building as his home on the west side of Marine Street from where O.C. White's now stands. He was a prominent merchant ship owner and building contractor. In fact, from the irregular sizes of many of the coquina blocks used in the construction, one would surmise that he used leftover building materials from other sites. Don Miguel lived in the house until 1799, when it was converted to one of St. Augustine's first hotels. It remained a hotel, variously known as the Union Hotel, Levington's, and Bridier's, until the mid-1800s. The hotel changed hands several times until Mrs. Margaret S. Worth, widow of General William Worth, a prominent military figure in the Mexican-American War, bought the house and turned it back into a residence.

Mrs. Worth lived there by herself and then with one of her daughters, Mary, and her husband, Colonel John Sprague, until she died in 1869. The house has since become known as the Worth Mansion. Another daughter, Margaret, then lived there following Mrs. Worth's death until a local cigar manufacturer bought it in 1904. George Potter, the one-time owner of Potter's Wax Museum, bought the building in 1948 and in 1961 moved it, stone by stone, to its present location. The former site of the house is now O.C. White's parking lot.

Dave White is a supercharged, frenetic entrepreneur. He bought the building in the early '90s and within a few short weeks, opened O.C. White's. "O.C." stands for "Out of Control," by the way.

The fire occurred on Friday the 13th of November 1992. The week before, one of Dave's purveyors gave him an old framed photograph of the Worth Mansion when it still sat on the west side of Marine Street. Dave had hung the picture in his office on the third floor. The fire started in the dish room below the office on the second floor. There was nothing much flammable in the dish room. It was just a small area where dishes, napkins, and flatware were kept so that the servers wouldn't have to go downstairs so often. At the end of the day, the room was emptied, and all the dishes, flatware, and napkins were taken downstairs.

However, despite the lack of flammable items, the fire was hot.

Not only did it blow out the second-floor windows, it shot straight up to the third floor and turned Dave's office to charcoal. "My desk looked like a huge charcoal briquette," Dave said afterward. The walls, the ceiling, and the floor were also charred, although the floor did not burn through, which was strange.

Even stranger, the picture of the Worth Mansion Dave had been given the week before, its paper backing, and the wall immediately around it were not burned. The unscathed picture still hangs on Dave's wall today with two or three very small heat blisters on the frame. Nor did anything happen to a silver candelabrum that was sitting on the floor. For several inches around the candelabra, the floor was untouched. TV security cameras, stereo speakers, and liquor bottles were melted, but nothing happened to the picture or the candelabra.

Dave didn't believe in ghosts before the fire, but he does now. He readily admits that the restaurant has several ghosts. It has even been featured on national television as the most haunted restaurant in the U.S. "Sometimes I'm sitting at my desk up on the third floor and this foul body odor fills the room, like some guy who hasn't had a bath in months. It'll linger for five or ten minutes and then disappear. And then it'll come back again. My oldest daughter won't even come up here by herself. And there's the door. This happens all the time. I go up the stairs, stick my key in the lock, and before I can even turn it, the door swings open six inches or so. Fifteen or twenty minutes later, I might go downstairs, and I always keep the office locked when no one's in it, and when I come back up, stick my key in the door, the thing swings open again. It's crazy.

"When it first started happening, I had the door rehung, replaced the lock and the deadbolt, and made sure everything was properly lined up. Makes no difference. I think old Mrs. Worth is doing it and she likes me. Doesn't want me to go to the trouble of having to unlock the door every time.

"I don't close very often myself anymore," Dave continued, "but when I did, I'd be sitting up in the office at 1:30 in the morning. No one is here. The building is locked tight. I'm counting my pennies, and I hear someone walking across the second-story wood floor below. Then, the footsteps start up the stairs—they're also wood. I go to the door, ask who's there. No one answers, so I lock up and go down to check it out. I go into the walk-in cooler, the dish room, the stalls, down on the first floor. There's nobody else in the building. Then I go back up and start counting. Bump, bump, bump. Footsteps on the wood floors again. There were times when I almost got some flour and spread it around to see if anyone was leaving tracks, but I got to where it didn't bother me all that much. I figured maybe it was Mrs. Worth kind of checking things out for me."

Things get moved around a lot, especially clothes and purses. And keys are a big item. Kathy, Dave's wife, and Julie, one of Dave's daughters, who manage the place, will leave keys in the office on the desk and minutes later can't find them. But they always turn up after an hour or so. Perhaps Mrs. Worth wants to make sure they stay around for a while.

A Jaguar head—this is Jacksonville Jaguar country—used to hang on the wall on the first floor, and there was an old ship's figurehead on the front wall on the second floor. One night, one of the servers hung a string of beads on the jaguar. The next day when the staff opened, the beads were hanging on the figurehead, so no one touched them. The following day, the beads were back on the jaguar. The beads get moved around often. Mrs. Worth is very playful.

One evening Julie and Tim were closing. It was two in the morning and it had been a long day. Everyone else had left and they had locked all the outside doors. They trudged up the stairs to the office together, counted the money, and locked it in the safe. As they left, locked the office, and started down the stairs, they heard the tinkling of wine glasses coming from the dish room. Julie and Tim looked at each other. They knew the dish room was empty. They went on down the stairs to the second floor and over to the beer closet. Tim glanced in the dish room just to make sure. It was definitely empty. Both of them were edgy now.

They both went into the beer closet so they could restock the bar downstairs. They had removed several cases and were standing outside the closet when suddenly the office door upstairs, which they had just locked, slammed shut. Julie screamed and jumped back into the beer closet.

Tim looked at her, "What the devil was that?"

"What do you think it was?" she shrieked. She was petrified.

When they had calmed themselves, they cautiously went to the bottom of the stairs to look up. There was nothing there.

"Forget the beer. Let's get out of here," Julie said, and they raced downstairs, set the alarm, locked the door, and left, not even bothering to turn off the lights. Julie was so scared she insisted that Tim follow her home.

Julie relates, "Before the fire the air conditioning unit was on the third floor, and we had to go up there to change the thermostat. There was only one key, and the on-duty manager had it. Well, it would be hot as blazes in the restaurant, so the manager would go up and adjust the thermostat to 65 or 70°. Then, five minutes later, it would be frigid, and when the manager would go up, the thermostat would be yanked all the way down to 50°. Back and forth, back and forth, 50° to 90° all night. And we know it wasn't anyone playing games, because there was only the one key."

Charley grew up in St. Augustine and has been at O.C. White's a long time. He won't admit to seeing anything, but he has smelled lots of strange smells, seen flashing lights, and heard things. One night he was closing up and had just walked the cleaning crew out. "We start locking up from the top down, so I went up to make sure the office door was locked and to turn the lights off on the way down. I had just about finished and was about ready to turn the alarm on when I heard this bam! bam! bam! on the second floor. I had no idea what it was so I ran up and found three different chairs at three different tables on the floor instead of upside down on the tables. And they didn't fall off; they were sitting upright on the floor. It was like someone had grabbed the chairs off the tables and slammed them down on the floor. I guess somebody wanted some service and wasn't ready to leave yet."

And one evening, not long after opening, Jennifer was serving a couple at one of the tables upstairs. She had just taken their order and turned to go when she saw the salt- and peppershakers on the next table start to dance. She gasped. Two other servers came over and the five of them, the three servers and the couple, watched as the shakers danced around the table, stopped, and started dancing again.

Shortly after Donna began working at the restaurant, she helped close. Each table has a candle and one of her duties was to go around and blow out all the candles. One afternoon she came in to open at 4:00, and when she went up to the second floor to start getting things ready, she noticed that one of the candles was burning—and she was the first one there. It couldn't have burned all night, she thought, because the candles weren't that big, and, besides, the closing manager would certainly have noticed when he locked up. She was so excited, she went back down to tell the others what had happened, but they just gave her a ho-hum look. "It happens all the time," one of them said.

Brandy was coming down the stairs one evening with several trays under her arm. "Something—it felt like of those hand buzzer things—zapped me right in the belly. I screamed, dropped the trays, and tripped down to the landing. Jeff and Vicki, two other servers who were downstairs, ran up to see what happened. I was okay, but, boy, was I scared."

The kitchen, too, has lots of activity. One of the prep cooks, Stephanie, came in early to get things ready. No one else was there yet. She got out the recipe book, which is a large three- or four-inch loose-leaf binder, and started to work. After a time she had to go to the restroom. When she returned, the recipe book was on the floor. All of the recipes had been taken out. A little unnerved, she put them all back and went back to work. A half hour later, she had to go up to the walk-in cooler. When she returned, the recipe book was back on the floor with all of the recipes out. That's when she went outside and waited for someone else to arrive.

The same sort of thing has happened to the chef, Cecil. The metal whisks are kept in a deep pan. There's no way they can fall out, but they flip out of the pan, and Cecil is constantly picking them off the floor. Pots and pans, too, inexplicably fall off their hooks. Cecil just shrugs and puts up with it.

And then there are the voices. Almost all of the employees at O.C. White's, even the new people, have had their names called out by an unknown voice. As Julie puts it, "I swear I'll be working with Morgan and hear her call my name, but when I turn around and say, 'What?' she just says, 'Huh? I didn't say anything.' It happens all the time."

The ghosts at O.C. White's must love it there. For one thing the food is excellent and on a chilly, fog-laden December evening, it's a wonderful place to sit with a glass of wine and stare out the window. Only watch out for the salt- and peppershakers.

THE KENWOOD

INN

*K*errianne Constant is Irish, very superstitious, and a bit otherworldly, attuned to the supernatural. Maybe that's why the spirits who live in the Kenwood Inn, which Kerrianne and her husband, Mark, have owned for the last sixteen years, are so comfortable and pleasant. Like Kerrianne and Mark, they are also very gracious and even warm—as warm as spirits can be.

The Kenwood Inn on Marine Street was built in 1865 as an inn. In 1885 an addition was made to the side of the building, and in 1910 a wing was added to the back. It has always been an inn, boarding house, or hotel, variously known by such names as the Kenwood Hotel, Mr. T's Boarding House, and the Kenwood Inn.

Mark and Kerrianne owned another inn in New Hampshire and had decided to move on. Kerrianne's intuitions are strong. She depends more on positive feelings than anything else. When she came to St. Augustine looking for property, she immediately fell in love with the city. She hadn't made reservations, but she called the Kenwood, then owned by Dick Smith, just to ask if he knew anyone who might be interested in selling. And, although the Kenwood wasn't for sale, she told Dick that if he were ever interested in selling to please let her know.

When she arrived and walked into the Kenwood to visit, however, she was overcome by an intense feeling. She knew that she had to buy the place. She hadn't even walked through and checked the plumbing or the wiring. Dick looked at her and simply said, "Yup." Kerrianne called Mark and told him that she thought she'd just bought an inn. That was in February. By April, Mark, Kerrianne, and daughter Caitlin were in the house. Perhaps it is telling that they have been at the Kenwood for sixteen years, when most inns and bed and breakfasts turn over every three or four years.

Mark didn't believe in anything supernatural and still has his doubts, but from the very beginning, Kerrianne has been aware of the spirits in the inn. A psychic toured the house and asked Kerrianne if she knew about Raymond. At that point, she did not. "Well," the psychic said, "he's very nice, and he loves you and your family a lot. He really likes what you've done to the inn. He followed me around and went in every room with me. He particularly likes Room # 7." When Mark and Kerrianne researched the history of the inn, they learned that a Raymond LaBorda owned the inn in 1886.

Raymond quickly made a name for himself. He was a great host. Guests reported folding up their comforters and placing them on a chair before going to sleep at night, only to awake in the morning covered by the same comforters. Raymond had tucked them in. And there are some folks from South Carolina who stay from time to time and who are very sensitive. When they come into the inn,

Raymond leads them up to their room like a good concierge.

Although he enjoys Room # 7, he also likes to keep his eye on who comes and goes, and he spends a lot of time sitting in the green-striped, upholstered armchair just inside the front door. There are days when Kerrianne has to straighten the upholstery every twenty or thirty minutes, because Raymond has wrinkled it by sitting in the chair. Of course, he's only being a good host, waiting by the door to welcome guests.

Raymond isn't all business. He likes to have his fun. The room lights, especially in Room # 8, get turned on and off in the middle of the night. Kerrianne doesn't want to make anyone nervous, so she'll say, "Well, perhaps a bulb was loose."

The guest will reply, "No, no. We were in bed asleep, when the lights were turned on, and we could see that the switch had been flipped on. Then, they were turned off."

And Raymond used to love to turn water on and off, especially in Room # 7, both in the sinks and the showers. He doesn't do it anymore. Maybe he was fascinated with indoor plumbing but now has lost interest.

He also loves to play with the answering machine, which, until recently, was on a counter next to a wall phone. The staff answers the phone between ten in the morning and ten at night, and lets the answering machine pick up any other calls at night and in the early morning. Raymond decided he liked these new-fangled machines. Between ten and ten-thirty every morning, there would be three messages on the answering machine: "If you'd like to make a call, please hang up and try again," this in spite of the fact that no one had used the phone and no incoming messages had been received. It drove Kerrianne crazy. She quickly realized that the message, "If you'd like to make a call, please hang up and try again," was only given when one tried to call out, so there was but one answer—Raymond.

The resident housekeepers, Bob and Gena, thought Kerrianne was a bit touched in the head, so she invited them to stand there and listen. Sure enough they got the "If you'd like to make a call . . . " message on the answering machine. "It's him," Kerrianne said. "It's him. I know it's him." Bob and Gena looked at each other in amazement.

In the middle of the second recording, Kerrianne stepped in front of the answering machine, put her arm around Raymond's shoulder, or where she thought his shoulder would be, and said, "Raymond, you've got to stop this."

The second message finished and the third came on. Raymond was having too much fun to pay any attention to Kerrianne. When the "If you'd like to make a call . . . " finished, however, the phone didn't hang up. It started beeping as if the phone were off the hook. "Oh, my gosh," Kerrianne gasped. "I'm standing on him." And she jumped back. As soon as she did, the beeping stopped. The phone was hung up. Bob and Gena were speechless.

Sometimes Raymond gets a little carried away. A guest once asked to stay in Raymond's room, Room #7. She talked about nothing except wanting to "experience" Raymond and then went off to see the sights in St. Augustine. When she came back, all three locks on the door to Room # 7 were frozen. Mark quickly replaced them and got the lady into her room. The staff laughed out back, because Raymond obviously didn't care for her and had locked her out. She didn't even realize she was "experiencing" him. That night she continued complaining about not having run into him. The next morning she left, and as soon as she was gone, the three locks on the front door froze.

But Raymond is not the only spirit in the place. Across the living room from Raymond's green chair there is a doorway leading out to the hall and the stairs. A ceramic angel flutters above the opening, heralding those who pass through. Mark, the skeptic, was sitting in Raymond's chair early one afternoon and suddenly saw a woman descending the stairs. She had long, dark hair and was wearing a flowing white dress. He knew she wasn't a guest, so he walked across the room to see who it was. No one was there.

Shortly thereafter, just after midnight a woman awakened a frequent guest of the inn and his wife and announced to them that her name was Lavender. She had long, dark hair and was wearing a flowing white dress. Then she disappeared. That room is now called Lavender's Room. More than once people have seen the woman getting out of bed in Room #14, and the housekeepers often find long, dark hairs in the bathtub in Room #15, even when no one has occupied the room or the occupant has been a bald man. As Kerrianne says, "Lavender sleeps in 14, bathes in 15 and then comes down for her little snack and to meet all the guests."

Another spirit is found on the third floor—an older, Victorian lady with piercing blue eyes, her hair in a tight bun. In December St. Augustine hosts a B&B tour. Each B&B is paired with a local restaurant, and visitors can visit all the establishments and sample the local cuisine. Last year a woman came running downstairs, excitedly asking if anyone had seen the ghost in Room # 17. She had just visited the room and was leaving when she happened to turn and see an older lady, sitting in a chair in the corner of the room. She had piercing blue eyes, her hair in a tight bun, and was wearing a Victorian suit.

The spirits that dwell in the Kenwood Inn seem to be a happy, peaceful lot and add to the ambiance. Those who are sensitive enough to feel or see them enjoy their company. And many writers who stay at the inn find that they easily overcome writers' block just sitting in the courtyard. Seventy-five percent of the inn's guests are repeat customers.

But Kerrianne worries. She and Mark are installing a sprinkler system on the third floor. Often major disturbances such as this can cause spirits to move on. Recently, another psychic stayed and reported to Mark and Kerrianne that one of their female spirits was getting ready to leave. She also mentioned that frequently, when spirits depart, they do a few mischievous things. Shortly thereafter, the third-floor alarm system activated. Repairmen spent two days investigating and could not find the cause.

Kerrianne hopes the spirits all stay, but if one of them has to go, she wishes her eternal rest.

THE OLDEST

HOUSE

*F*or those sensitive enough to feel it, the first floor of the Oldest House is mildly unsettling. The house was built around 1723 when Maria Francisca Guevara y Domínguez, a local girl whose mother was a third-generation St. Augustinian, married Tomás González y Hernández, a former sailor from Tenerife in the Canary Islands. He became an artilleryman in St. Augustine and could not have afforded such a house, so it probably was a dowry gift from Maria Francisca's parents. Tomás and Maria Francisca had eleven children, six of whom died, their memories forever imbedded within the walls of 14 St. Francis Street.

At the time, the Oldest House was at the south end of town, across the street from the Franciscan monastery, the Monastery of the Immaculate Conception. Burials were conducted either there in the monastery chapel or up on the plaza at the parish church. Records show that most burials were in the monastery where Hipólito González served as an acolyte, so the González family was well acquainted with death.

Life in the remote outpost of St. Augustine was harsh. Pirates and British troops raided from time to time—in 1740 British General James Oglethorpe laid siege to the town for thirty days. Hurricanes flooded the area. Droughts dried up crops. Dampness or insects often ruined what food there might have been.

But the González family endured and remained in their little two-room house. In 1747 Tomás was transferred from the artillery to an infantry company and in 1758, at age 57, retired from active service. It should have been time for Tomás and Maria to enjoy their old age in the comfort and care of their children. But that was not to be.

In 1763 Florida became a British colony, and the family left for a new life in Cuba. The house sat empty for some time under the care of Jesse Fish, who was a property manager, until 1775 when Joseph Peavitt bought it. He was the paymaster for the East Florida British troops. He had married Mary Evans Fenwick, whose first husband, also a British soldier, had died.

Shortly after purchasing the house, they added a second story and a fireplace in the east room, and it became a store and tavern catering to the British troops quartered in what had been the monastery across the street. In 1779 Peavitt left the army to tend to his businesses, and Mary became a successful midwife. During the Revolutionary War the inn must have been a hot spot of social activity with all the newly arrived refugees from the north.

The Spanish regained possession of Florida in 1783, but Peavitt, who was Roman Catholic, decided to remain because he owned several thousand acres, houses and farm buildings, and many slaves, horses, and cows. And, of course, he and Mary still maintained their inn on St. Francis Street and lived around the corner on Marine Street. Under the Spanish they continued to prosper, and when Joseph died in April of 1786, Mary was a rich widow.

Mary's choice for a third husband was not a good one. John Hudson was a rounder, given to heavy drinking, gambling, and lavish spending. He was twenty-eight years younger than Mary, which itself was not unusual for the times. In fact, in the census of 1786, only 109 married couples were recorded. Twenty-five of the wives were forty or over, and eleven of those were married to men seven or more years their junior.

Within two years Hudson had run up such heavy debts that Mary's estate was in a shambles, and the house on St. Francis Street, as well as most of their other holdings and possessions, was auctioned off.

Gerónimo Álvarez, newly arrived from Spain, became the new owner. He also bought the Tovar House next door, built before 1763, and in 1788 married Antonia Venz, a young Minorcan. Gerónimo did well as a baker, storekeeper, and landowner. So did his son, Antonio. In 1812 Gerónimo became the first elected mayor of St. Augustine and was also the senior warden, the lay leader, of the local parish church. Antonio was the acting secretary of the City Council.

After the deaths of his parents, Antonio and his family continued to live in the house, which remained in the family for ninety-two years until the Álvarez descendants sold it in 1882.

Dr. C. P. Carver bought the house in 1884 and made major renovations to it, adding a round tower to the northeast corner and life-size statues of the Four Seasons in the garden. During Dr. Carver's ownership the house became known as "The Oldest House." Dr. Carver was a dentist and was continually being disturbed in his practice by tourists wishing to see his home, so he started charging admission to discourage the visitors. But interest remained high, and by 1892 the house was open for viewing in January, February, and March. Eventually Mrs. Carver died in the house, where her funeral was also held.

The Oldest House next passed to Judge and Mrs. James W. Henderson, but death and tragedy were again to hit the house. On Friday, July 10, 1903, Joe Williams, the caretaker, came home after spending the evening with friends at a local bar. While getting ready for bed he attempted to pull the hammer of his loaded pistol to the half-cocked position and pulled it back too far. The pistol slipped in his hands and discharged, hitting his wife in the side. The metal stays of her corset were driven into her intestines, and she died not long after.

In 1918 the St. Augustine Historical Society, which had been formed in 1882, acquired the house. The Society began a program to restore it as much as possible to its "original and ancient condition." Today, thanks to the Historical Society, "The Oldest House" presents a unique window into St. Augustine's colorful past.

With its wonderful history, what about the ghosts? "The Oldest House" has seen so much tragedy and death over its centuries of existence. Reis Libby has been at the Historical Society and the Oldest House in a variety of positions for over twenty years and knows the place well. He won't admit to seeing any ghosts, but many times he sees things out of the corner of his eye. Objects get moved around in the house, books and small objects are moved from place to place, chairs are turned, and there is that uncomfortable feeling on the first floor. He doesn't like to go up in the attic of the Tovar House either.

During one period of restoration Reis also found little blue seed beads, typical of the First Spanish Period, imbedded in a coquina wall, a place not accessible to humans after the wall was built. Because many occupants had slaves in the early history of the house, could the beads have been put there during construction for some shamanistic reason? Blue is a very symbolic color in many religions, especially Santeria, which came from Africa to Cuba in the slave trade.

With permission from the Historical Society, Joanne, my sensitive friend, toured the buildings and grounds after hours. Sitting quietly upstairs in the bedroom, she sensed a woman, a black servant, apparently waiting for her mistress. Was she Mary Peavitt's nurse, Isabel, or was she Joe Williams's wife waiting for her husband on that ill-fated evening? Joanne was not disturbed by this presence, which walked from time to time to the window and mirror on the south wall and stood for a while in the northwest corner of the room. Joanne also came in contact with the presence that Reis felt uncomfortable around while in the attic of the Tovar House. Other than these, the site is surprisingly clear of paranormal activity.

Regardless, the Oldest House is a fascinating place and offers us a rare opportunity to look into the past and to be enveloped by almost four hundred years of history.

GHOST MAGNETS

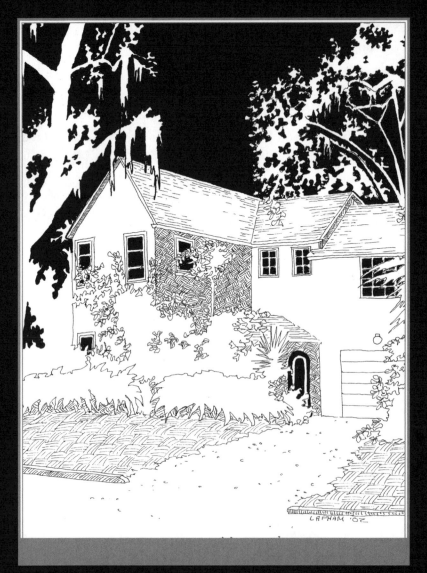

*M*ost of us have witnessed something unexplainable—a feeling that someone else was present when we were alone, a distinctive fragrance that had no source, an enveloping warmth on a cold day or a frigid blast on a warm one, a securely hung picture falling from a wall for no reason. Some have heard footsteps, seen movement or lights where there were none, even felt the grasp of a nonexistent hand. A few of us may have actually seen ghosts or heard them speak.

But there are a very, very few who encounter these supernatural phenomena on an almost daily basis, psychics who have the gift of sensitivity. They are magnets and even though they may have no desire to consort with the spirit world, they must daily confront these unwanted contacts.

Joanne and Pat are such a couple. Both are extremely sensitive. Pat is a Celt and has experiences on a daily basis. Joanne also comes from Celtic stock and the mysticism often associated with the Celts was significant from early childhood. "I remember hands grasping my shoulder, footsteps following me around. I would be enveloped by cold air that would stay with me even when I moved from one place to another, and all sorts of strange things went on in my bedroom which I never really minded or even thought unusual," Joanne relates.

Joanne grew up in a rambling, old Florida house, which her grandfather had purchased in 1941. Joanne's room on the second floor looked like any other child's room—a bed, dresser, desk, and a rocker. Crafted in the 1800s, the chair has been passed down from generation to generation, from her great-grandmother to her grandfather's sister to her when she was in second grade. Oddly, the rocker rocked by itself all the time (and still does to this day). Joanne also had a mobile hanging from the ceiling. It, too, swayed back and forth, even when the air was absolutely still. Then there was the door. It opened by itself even though it was hung perfectly and the latch was seated correctly. As a teenager, when privacy can be so important, Joanne finally had her father install a padlock to the keep the door closed. It was marginally effective.

During her college years, Joanne brought her roommate home to Florida one weekend. At the time her parents were living in Tennessee, and her grandfather and his new wife, who felt too uncomfortable to live in the house, had another place nearby. So Grandfather had loaned the homestead to a missionary couple back in the States on sabbatical. However, Joanne was allowed access to the house and maintained her room upstairs.

Joanne's roommate, Sue, didn't believe in ghosts. She didn't believe in anything otherworldly. In fact, she was an atheist, and decidedly not religious. Religious people made her nervous, and she didn't like to be around them. When Joanne had told Sue that a missionary couple was living in the house, she almost hadn't come.

Consequently, when they arrived, Joanne hurried through the introductions as quickly as she could and rushed Sue upstairs.

Joanne had left her room pretty much as it had been when she graduated from high school, and, of course, her beloved rocker was still there. She let Sue have the room and put her own things in the guest room next door. She had always taken the peculiarities of the room so much for granted that she didn't even mention them to Sue. The girls quickly unpacked and then were off to see Joanne's grandfather—being careful to stay as clear of the missionaries as possible, for Sue's sake.

When Joanne and Sue arrived at her grandfather's house, they had a wonderful visit. The following day he invited the two girls to dinner and a movie in the early evening. When it came time to go, Sue wasn't feeling well and decided to stay home. She went upstairs to lie down as soon as Joanne left.

Sue closed the door, took her shoes off, turned back the bedspread, and lay down. When she closed her eyes her head swam, but she kept them closed, and soon she was asleep. Sometime later, Sue woke with a start. It was almost dark, but she could see an older woman sitting in the rocking chair with her back to Sue. At first Sue thought it was the missionary's wife and was offended by the invasion of privacy.

"What are you doing here?" she demanded.

The old lady didn't say anything. She just turned slowly and looked over her shoulder at Sue, expressionless. Sue had never laid eyes on this woman before, and the realization of what she was seeing suddenly hit her. She bounded off the bed, ran towards the door, and flicked on the light. The old woman vanished.

When Joanne returned a short time later, Sue was sitting in the living room with the missionaries. As Joanne entered, Sue rushed to her gasping, "Oh, Joanne, I'm so glad to see you!" She immediately pulled her upstairs to the room Joanne was using—Sue wouldn't go into her own room. She related what had happened and was so frightened that she slept in the guest room with Joanne for the rest of her visit.

As Joanne recalls, "After we went back to school she told everyone for the rest of the year that I lived in a haunted house and she never would come home with me again."

Joanne and Pat took possession of her grandfather's house on the first of April 1993, April Fool's Day. There was a full moon. They laughed about it later; what a fitting time to return to this house. From the very first strange things happened. They saw and heard doors slam and heard footsteps at odd hours. A room air conditioner inexplicably came on even in winter when it was not plugged in, and file cabinet doors opened and closed of their own accord. One of the first things Pat did in the house was to renovate the library. During the many hours he spent in the room he heard strange noises and saw shadows duck behind furniture and boxes. He even saw the old lady Joanne's roommate, Sue, had seen fifteen years earlier. And, most astonishing, he met and talked to an older gentleman who might have been Joanne's great-grandfather, William, who had occupied Joanne's room and died there before she was born.

These kinds of encounters have happened to both Joanne and Pat all their lives, so it wasn't surprising recently when Pat, Joanne, and daughter Miranda had an encounter along St. George Street. It was a beautiful, clear, warm afternoon about five o'clock, and they had gone out for a walk—Joanne wanted to take some pictures of the "Governor's" house at 214 St. George Street. This house is informally known as the "Governor's" because the most prominent ghost there is a former Spanish governor (see the "Gallant Governor" story in *Ghosts of St. Augustine*). Because the sidewalk was so narrow, Pat was walking several steps ahead.

Joanne stopped for a moment at 224 St. George, thinking she might have written down the wrong number, just as Pat passed by the parking lot which separates the two houses. Seeing the 214 house number, he turned back to tell Joanne that he had found the right place. As he turned, he suddenly saw a strange-looking man walking quickly up the street directly behind Miranda and Joanne. The man was about five feet eight or nine inches tall with dark hair. He wore a light brown coat with wide lapels. Pat started to tell Joanne to move out of the way of this approaching person, when the man disappeared right in front of Pat's eyes. Pat decided that he must have imagined seeing the figure, so he didn't say anything.

At the same instant, Miranda, who was closest to the street, fell violently to the pavement, even though Joanne had been holding her hand tightly. Joanne saw no one else on the street. She later related, "Suddenly, I felt her kind of jerk forward. Her hand slipped out of mine and the next thing I knew, poor Miranda was on her hands and knees, crying and bleeding from her fall on the sidewalk. For some odd reason, I was suddenly filled with rage, not at Miranda, but at everything in general. I felt like cursing something. Pat ran toward us and asked what happened. Still filled with my unexplainable rage, I snapped, 'What do you think happened? She fell!' "

Miranda wasn't badly hurt. Joanne promptly sat her on a low wall and put Neosporin and band-aids on her knees and elbows. Pat held sobbing Miranda to comfort her. Just then, Joanne looked up and noticed that the Governor's house was right in front of her. 'I wonder . . . ,' she thought. Then she looked more closely at Miranda's injuries. Only her knees and hands were scraped. Oddly, her toes weren't. She was wearing open-toed sandals with no socks, and if she had tripped and fallen, her toes most certainly would have been skinned and her sandals scuffed. Besides, that area of the sidewalk was smooth. All this went through her mind, but she didn't say anything. She just took several photos of the house then continued their walk.

That evening as they were driving home, Joanne talked about the day's events while Miranda slept in the back seat, and she mentioned to Pat, "You know, I'm probably just over-reacting, but I can't help wondering if our being near that house had something supernatural to do with Miranda's fall." Pat turned a little pale, then replied, "I didn't want to tell you this at the time, but let me tell you what I saw . . . " Pat then told Joanne about the disappearing man. Joanne started to understand the reason for her sudden maternal rage at nothing in particular. She was angry with a ghost. "How dare he pick on an innocent little girl."

When they got back home and Joanne was getting Miranda ready for her bath, she casually asked her if she remembered her fall that afternoon. "Yes," Miranda answered. "I got boo-boos and lots of band-aids." Miranda loved her band-aids. Joanne asked her what happened and Miranda replied that she had been pushed.

"Pushed? Who pushed you?"

"That mean man. He pushed me hard," and she pointed to the small of her back. For several weeks after the incident, Joan asked Miranda about the incident, and the little girl consistently answered, "That mean man pushed me."

But that's not the end of the story. Later, Joanne and Pat were visiting the Old St. Augustine Village. They were talking to one of the workers and the subject of ghosts came up. Astonishingly, the workman related seeing a strange-looking man on the grounds. He was about five feet eight or nine inches tall with dark hair. He wore a very old-fashioned, light brown coat with wide lapels, and he disappeared as suddenly as he had appeared.

Joanne is still furious that anyone, even a ghost, would pick on her child. She is a very spunky woman and often goes by herself down St. George Street hoping to confront the being that pushed Miranda. She is such a ghost magnet, I'm sure the hapless wretch will one day blunder into her path.

OLD ST. AUGUSTINE

VILLAGE

South of the Plaza lies of one St. Augustine's oldest sites, Old St. Augustine Village. Bounded by St. George, Bridge, Cordova, and Palm Row, Old St. Augustine Village provides a rare look into four centuries of Ancient City history. The site was included in the town plan in 1572. In the northeast corner of the Village there is evidence of a sixteenth-century Spanish church, a cemetery, and a hospital. To the southeast are the remains of the bridge, which once crossed over Maria Sanchez Creek, and a portion of the eighteenth-century Spanish Colonial defense line. President Lincoln's 1863 Emancipation Proclamation, freeing the slaves, was read to the public on nearby grounds.

Nothing remains of the oldest structures, of course, except archeological evidence—and, for those who can hear, the sounds of over four hundred years of life and death and suffering in the America's oldest city. But historic structures do exist there. The

Village is a collection of nine houses spanning the period from 1790 to 1910.

In 1941 Mr. Kenneth Dow purchased the Prince Murat House on the corner of St. George and Bridge Streets. Within ten years he had acquired all nine buildings in the area. Mr. Dow was an antique collector and over the years obtained antiques from all over the world, much of it finding its way to what is now Old St. Augustine Village. In 1989, he donated the entire block with the nine houses and many of his collections of antiques, art, and heirlooms to the Museum of Arts and Sciences in Daytona Beach, which began the work of creating what is today the museum of Old St. Augustine Village. The buildings have been rehabilitated to house exhibit galleries featuring Dow's collections and to depict life during various periods of the last four centuries. It took eleven years to complete the project and to make the houses accessible to the public.

The Murat House is the oldest in the Village, built about 1790. Shortly after it was finished, Antonio Canova purchased the house. The Canova family owned the home until 1877 and told the story that in 1824 they had rented the house for several months to Prince Achille Murat, nephew of Napoleon Bonaparte, who was quite a celebrity at the time. The house is built of coquina and originally had two rooms on the street with a loggia in back, typical of Spanish homes of the time. There would also have been a separate kitchen behind the house. There was a small addition in the 1890s, and Mr. Dow added a kitchen and rooms to the back of the house. Interestingly, a musket ball is imbedded in what was the original outside west wall.

Because of the story about Prince Murat, the house became known as the Murat House, and Mr. Dow traveled to Paris to collect French Empire furniture for the home. In the late 1940s he opened a small antique shop in the house and wrote an article about his collection in *Antique Magazine*. The building today reflects Mr. Dow's house as he furnished it with early American and French Empire Period antiques suited for the lifestyle of a prince.

Around 1839 the Canova family built the Canova House and the little yellow structure, which originally sat next to the Murat on St. George Street. It was the home of John Canova for many years during the 1800s. In 1905 Mary Hayden, a wealthy hotel owner, bought both the Murat and the yellow house, which she moved to its current location. In its place and on the lot next to it on St. George Street she built the two large Colonial Revival structures. Mary and her daughter, Nellie, lived at first in the pink Murat House while they renovated and upgraded the little yellow structure as a winter cottage.

When Mr. Dow bought the yellow house he promised long-time resident Sarah McKinnon that she could remain in the house for as long as she lived. She must have loved the place because she lived to be over 102. I know no one who has seen or experienced her, but I'm willing to bet her spirit is hanging around the home.

Emmanuel de Medicis was a dry goods merchant. In 1899 he owned the Canova House, which he turned into a boarding house, and built the store next door on the corner of Bridge and Cordova Streets. Mr. de Medicis had a huge family of seven daughters and seems to have had trouble housing all of them. In 1921 he converted the store into two three-room apartments for two of his daughters' families.

Of the newer homes on the site, the Worcester House is, perhaps, the most interesting. It was constructed in 1904 by a local resident, Mr. John L. Henry, and has been carefully exhibited with an Edwardian interior. Today the house boasts gas lighting, a coal-burning stove, an icebox, and an 1885 steam washing machine. The home even has a game room and indoor bathrooms. During the rehabilitation the staff found a fragment of a wall sconce fixture, and contacted some Victorian Period lighting experts, who found matching fixtures. This is but one example of the attention to detail that has gone into rehabilitating the homes.

And what of ghosts in the Old St. Augustine Village? There must be a presence or two here, one of the oldest areas of the city.

During the early development of the museum, the project manager maintained offices in the top floor of the Murat House. One night Greg, a staff member, was working late upstairs when he heard the front door open. Now, if you've spent any time at all in St. Augustine you know that nothing much goes on before nine in the morning or after seven or eight in the evening, and especially south of the plaza, a mostly residential area. So Greg was surprised and a little alarmed when he heard the door open. Getting up from his work, he went quickly down the stairs to what was once the loggia and into the front of the house where he stopped cold. The front door had indeed opened and standing before him was a short man dressed in late eighteenth-century or early nineteenth-century clothing, looking somewhat confused by Greg's appearance. He shut the door behind himself and looked again at Greg. "May I help you?" Greg asked, thinking perhaps the man was a re-enactor or a tour guide of some sort, a not-uncommon sight in St. Augustine. The man instantly evaporated from sight. Stunned, Greg walked over to the door and checked it. It was locked. Finally, realizing what he'd just seen, he hurried back upstairs, turned off the lights and left

A paranormal research team some months ago investigated Old St. Augustine Village and two of the team members were standing on the second floor waiting for the others to come up. They heard footsteps in one of the rooms and at first thought someone else was up there with them. They walked into the other room and then into all the rooms on the second floor. No one was there. They never did determine who it was.

The research team picked up numerous presences on their electro-magnetic meters and took several photographs of orbs in many of the houses, but those who have worked there are reluctant to talk much about it. But, as old as the site is, how could it not be haunted? Tom Muir, the present director of Old St. Augustine Village, doesn't really believe in ghosts. He actually doesn't care one way or the other. He is interested only in the history of the site. He is passionate about it. Nowhere else in St. Augustine can you find so much history in such a small area. It is also a lovely place just to visit and rest a while in one of the many shaded nooks and crannies. It is a most unusual museum, and, if you listen carefully, I'm sure the ghosts who live there will enliven your tour.

 ANKSVILLE

CEMETERY

St. Augustine is well aware of its rich and colorful past, and many organizations work hard to preserve its heritage and record its history, among them the St. Augustine Genealogical Society. In recent years the society undertook the project of researching all the cemeteries in the area. Louis Sanks was a member of the society, one of the few men in the group and the only black man. Intensely interested in the history of the area, he was well thought of by everyone in the organization.

During the course of his research, Mr. Sanks learned that he actually owned the Sanksville Cemetery a short way out of town near Bakersville. The cemetery has a long but obscure history and was quite overgrown and in a state of decay. In the past whites had been buried in the front part of the cemetery, and, times being what they were, blacks were buried in the back. A falling-down, rusty, wrought iron fence separated the two areas. Mr. Sanks was so enthusiastic about Sanksville that Gay Rawley and

Karen Harvey, both members of the Genealogical Society, who had been assigned to research the cemeteries in the area anyway, agreed to help him research Sanksville. They became good friends, and Mr. Sanks called Gay his "cemetery historian" and Karen the "little lady from the grave." Their efforts involved listing the data on each gravestone, checking government records, and, where possible, interviewing descendants to gather historical information.

When Louis discovered that he owned the cemetery, he became determined to restore it, and Gay and Karen both offered to assist. He planned to rebuild the road, which led from the highway up along the side of the cemetery, reposition toppled gravestones, and spruce the place up. One day while he and Gay were working in the cemetery, Gay noticed that he seemed preoccupied.

"What's the matter, Mr. Sanks? You seem upset about something."

He stopped what he was doing and leaned on his shovel for a few moments, pondering. "You know, Missy, I know you well enough. I want to ask you something. Do you think it'd be wrong if I took that old fence down?"

Gay looked around. "What fence do you mean, Mr. Sanks?"

"Well, that one over there," he said, pointing to the fence running across the middle separating the front from the back part of the cemetery.

"Oh, Mr. Sanks. That fence is already almost down. Look at it. It's all broken and rusty. I don't see any reason why you can't remove it. Of course, you can," she replied, wondering why he was so worried.

"But you don't understand, Missy. White people built that fence to separate them from the back. We were supposed to stay in the back. It separated us, and maybe it's illegal for me to take it out."

"Oh, Mr. Sanks, that was a long time ago. It's not that way now.

Look at the two of us here working together. And, after all, it's your cemetery. You own it and you can do anything you please. If you want to take it out, take it out," Gay countered.

And so Mr. Sanks started to lift out the broken pieces of the fence and pull up those that were still anchored in the ground, piling them up near the perimeter. Just at that moment, Gay looked across the cemetery and saw two figures. Their appearance shocked her at first, but then she realized they were ghosts, a man and a woman, looking sad and bedraggled. They looked like Crackers from a hundred years ago. The slightly built woman wore a long blue dress with little flowers on it. It was obviously handmade, probably out of feed sacks. She had brown hair pulled back and tied in a tight bun. The man was short and stocky and wore a cheap wool suit, also obviously handmade, with large buttons. His hair was sandy yellow, and the sunlight shone on his big work-reddened hands. Neither the man nor the woman was smiling.

Mr. Sanks eyed her. "What are you looking at?"

"I'm looking at them," and she pointed at the two spirits. "Can you see them, Mr. Sanks?"

Turning, he replied nervously, "Yes, I see them. I see them. I can see his big, red hands. They're lost souls, and they don't like me tearing down this fence. They're probably the ones who built it."

"Oh, pooh, Mr. Sanks. They're not mad at you. They're just sorry. They're sorry they ever built that fence."

*   *   *   *   *

A couple of years later Mr. Sanks died, and his wife called Gay to ask her to give a eulogy at his funeral in the Methodist Church. "He specifically wanted you to tell the story of the two spirits in the Sanksville Cemetery."

"Mercy, Mrs. Sanks, I can't get up in front of all those people and tell that story."

"But he really wanted you to do that, Mrs. Rawley. I don't know why, but he really wanted you to tell that story at his funeral."

Of course, Gay was going to the funeral anyway, so she finally agreed to do it. Most of the members of the Society also attended the funeral, among them Karen, Carol, and Margie, and other friends from the Genealogical Society. They all went to the big, beautiful church on King St. to pay their last respects to their old friend. At the appointed time Gay walked up to the lectern and related the story about seeing the ghosts in the Sanksville Cemetery. Then, as Mr. Sanks had requested, the whole congregation, white and black alike, went to the cemetery for the burial.

Later in the day, Gay, Karen, Carol, and Margie all felt the urge to return to the cemetery to be with their friend, Mr. Sanks. They were still very upset. When they got to the cemetery, they all gathered around his grave. Shortly afterward, a car pulled up, and there was Mrs. Sanks. The ladies were a bit embarrassed.

Gay said, "Oh, Mrs. Sanks, I'm sorry for invading your privacy by coming here like this."

"No, no," she replied. "You all loved Louis, and I'm so proud. You were his close friends."

Again forming a circle around the grave, all the women held tightly to one another. Just then, off to the side, appeared a man and a woman. They looked like Crackers from a hundred years ago. The slightly built woman wore a long blue dress with little flowers on it. It was obviously handmade, probably out of feed sacks. She had brown hair pulled back and tied in a tight bun. The man was short and stocky and wore a cheap wool suit, also obviously handmade, with large buttons. His hair was sandy yellow, and the sunlight shone on his big work-reddened hands. They were smiling.

THE WARRIORS

OF MOULTRIE CREEK

*M*oultrie Creek is a small stream off the Matanzas River just to the south of St. Augustine. It is tidal water, not navigable in many places except at high tide, a large plain of salt and cord grasses with mangrove swamps and marsh elders along the shores. Up the banks on drier ground, piney woods and palmettos blanket the land. Moultrie Creek is an out-of-the-way place. It always has been.

The area also has a dark history. The United States acquired Florida from Spain in 1821, and from the beginning, the indigenous Native Americans were trouble. The problem, of course, was that the Americans wanted the tribal land. Hoards of whites crowded into Florida, increasingly intruding on the Native Americans and taking their territory. Finally, in 1823 representatives of the United States government and most of the tribes of Florida signed the Treaty of Moultrie Creek. The Native Americans gave up much of their land in return for a four-million-acre reservation in the middle of the state. The Government also promised an Indian agency and blacksmith, along with annuities of livestock, food, supplies, and cash for twenty years. The United States never lived up to its promises and there followed many years of war.

General Thomas Jesup established Ft. Peyton a short distance southwest of St. Augustine in 1837. After he failed to round up the renegade Indians by negotiations in the summer, he decided on another tactic. He arranged for peace talks under a white flag of truce. In October General Joseph Hernandez, a native-born St. Augustinian, took 250 troops and met with the Chiefs Osceola and Coa Hadjo at Moultrie Creek. General Jesup, waiting up the road at Ft. Peyton, and General Hernandez had no intention of negotiating a peace. Their troops broke the truce and took the Native Americans prisoner, seventy-five warriors and six women. Among them were Osceola and Coa Hadjo. General Jesup was never able to recover from the stigma of breaking the truce with Osceola.

Through the years Moultrie Creek continued to be an out-of-the-way place. Even well into the twentieth century, a trip to St. Augustine was a long, arduous wagon ride. But the folk who lived along the creek were resilient Crackers, who sacrificed more than their share during the Civil War, the Spanish-American War, and all the wars since.

John Penn was one of those who had made such a sacrifice. He lived on an arm of Moultrie Creek and owned the land on both sides of it. Legally, the water in the arm was public, but few ever ventured up it—at least not after the Second World War. Penn had been severely wounded in France and had lost the lower part of his left arm. Machine-gunfire also had shattered his right knee so that he walked with a pronounced limp. But even worse, while he was fighting in Europe, his young wife had been raped and murdered along with their young son. John Penn was a bitter man and few braved the waters and John Penn's buckshot in Penn's slough.

Two who did were Jimmy Pardo and Nick Solano. Jimmy and Nick were best friends and inseparable from an early age. They both lived on the north side of Moultrie Creek and, like most kids there, when they weren't in school they were hunting and fishing. One of their favorite fishing spots was the water that sliced John Penn's property in two. But fishing there took stealth and caution. More than once John Penn had fired buckshot or rock salt at them with his twelve-gauge, and they had learned to be very careful. Even with half an arm and his gimpy walk he was a good shot and had peppered them more often than they had cared to be peppered with rock salt and BBs. They had learned over the years that an early morning high tide was the best time to fish, just before daylight. Mr. Penn was never up at that hour and the fishing was good.

Nick and Jimmy weathered the stings of Mr. Penn's twelve gauge and grew up to be fine young men, learning a few skills in the process. After high school both enlisted in the Marines and became tankers.

And then came the first Gulf War. Even in the Marines, Jimmy and Nick managed to stay together and were in the same tank crew in the First Platoon, Company A, Second Tank Battalion. Being the aggressive, confident men they were, they loved the war. Their company was in the thick of fighting and destroyed several units of the Republican Guard. When they came back to Camp Lejeune, North Carolina, their home base, they were decorated heroes.

Shortly after they returned, they both took leave and came home to St. Augustine for a well-deserved vacation. Of course, they fished as often as they could, and one night, after they'd covered all of their hot spots in the river and bay, they sat on Nick's porch drinking a beer and looked at each other with a shared idea.

"So, when are we going to hit Penn's place?"

"Hey, I don't know, man. What do you think?"

"Tide's about right in the morning, and we have to go back early next week. Might not get another chance."

"Tomorrow it is." And they clanked beer bottles in a toast of commitment. After the war, what could be so bad about a little rock salt?

The next morning at three they headed down to the dock and got into Nick's skiff and started the electric motor. Stealth was essential. The air was fresh, the sky clear, and the half moon, which was close to setting, gave just enough light to see by. Without a word Jimmy cast off, and they motored towards Penn's.

The water had almost reached flood tide as they entered the branch cutting into Penn's land. As they always did, one of them fished while the other maneuvered the skiff. Nick slowed the boat as Jimmy quietly got his rod ready and started casting.

Slowly they worked their way up the arm, Nick keeping the boat in the middle and Jimmy concentrating on his fishing. On the second or third cast, Jimmy hooked a nice red and landed it, trying to be as still as possible. Fishing was going to be good. Jimmy caught two more and motioned for Nick to switch with him.

Nick, too, immediately caught fish. It was exciting, and they both had a hard time containing themselves in their enthusiasm. They continued working slowly up the branch, totally absorbed in what they were doing, when suddenly someone yelled from the shore, "Hey, what are you boys doing?"

They both froze. Mr. John Penn. Jimmy turned off the electric motor and looked toward the shore. There, Penn stood behind a low palmetto, barely visible in the shadow of a pine tree.

"Look, Nick," Jimmy said in a low voice, "he's got a left arm and hand. Must be a prosthesis. It looks like he's holding his shotgun with both hands."

"That's really weird. He is using both hands. Must be some

kind of high-tech arm to do that."

Both were trying to think fast. Mr. Penn was walking toward the bank—and he wasn't limping. They had few options. The boat was closer to Penn than it was to the opposite bank, and, anyway, the electric motor wasn't that fast, not as fast as Penn's rock salt. They both privately hoped it was rock salt and not buckshot.

"I guess the only thing we can do is sit here and wait to see what happens."

"Hey, pal, when he lowers the muzzle of that shotgun, I'm going into the water."

"Yeah, I guess you're right. I'll go in from back here, so I can steer the motor. We'll just have to hope he doesn't have buckshot."

Mr. Penn stood motionless on the bank and smiled at them, "You boys catching anything?"

"Look, Jimmy, he's smiling at us. Guess he knows he has us cold," whispered Nick.

"Well, uh, yes sir. Got a nice mess of reds and some trout. Would you like some?" Nick thought placating him with a few fish might help.

"Why, I surely would. Much obliged." He set the butt of his shotgun down on the ground.

Nick turned on the electric motor and headed the bow of the boat to the bank. Jimmy got a stringer and started stringing fish.

"Two's enough, boys. That'll last me three or four days. I really appreciate this." As the bow bumped the shore, he stretched out his left arm and accepted the fish that Jimmy passed up to him. That's one heck of prosthesis, Jimmy thought.

"Well, thanks again for these fish. You boys better get back to fishing. Tide'll be turning soon. Good to see you again," and he turned and melted back into the shadows towards his darkened house.

Jimmy and Nick sat stunned. Neither moved or said anything for several minutes.

"Man, can you believe that? I wonder what came over him."

"Yeah, and that arm. Can you believe he was able to hold those fish with his left hand? And he wasn't limping either. Very strange."

"This is really weird. Wait'll the old man hears about this."

"I still can't believe he didn't blow us out of the water."

"Yeah, we are two lucky dudes."

"Hey, it's our Gulf War luck, buddy. We can't die." They both laughed.

By now the tide had started to turn, and neither of them were any longer interested in fishing. They turned the skiff and headed back to Nick's dock.

"Stay for breakfast, Jimmy. Dad will love to hear this." They both went up to the house and made coffee.

Nick's mom came into the kitchen a little while later to start breakfast. She was happy to see them. "Well, good morning, boys. How was the fishing?"

"Really good, Mom," Nick replied. He didn't say anything about Mr. Penn. Not yet. He wanted his dad to be there.

The smell of coffee, bacon, eggs, grits, and biscuits soon filled the house, and Nick's dad stumbled in, sleepy-eyed.

"Well, hey there, boys. You're up early."

"We went fishing, Dad."

They all sat down to eat. "Where'd you go? Have any luck?"

"We went over to Penn's, and, yes, we caught a lot of fish." Mr. Solano didn't react at all to that. Nick and Jimmy glanced at each other.

"A really weird thing happened. We ran into Mr. Penn."

Now, both of Nick's parents stared at Nick and shot looks at each other.

"Oh?" Mr. Solano asked in a tone of disbelief.

"Yeah, really weird. First of all, he was real friendly to us. And what was really strange was that he didn't walk with a limp, and when we offered him some fish, he took them from us with his left hand! He must have got one heck of a prosthesis while we were gone." Nick and Jimmy both chuckled.

Nick's mom and dad stared at him. "Are you sure it was Mr. Penn, Nick?"

"Of course, Dad, both of us saw him. He was standing on the bank right in front of us, and Jimmy handed him the fish. It was dark, but we could see it was Mr. Penn. And he sounded like Mr. Penn. Right, Jimmy?"

"Sure did. It was Mr. Penn, all right. But that artificial left arm sure was something. I couldn't believe it worked so well. And walking without a limp. Man."

"Yeah, that was as much of a surprise as his being nice to us and not shooting at us. He did have his shotgun with him."

Nick's dad sat back in his chair and smiled. "Well, I have an even bigger surprise for you boys. If you saw Mr. Penn this morning, you were looking at a ghost. Penn died six months ago."

Nick and Jimmy almost fell out of their chairs. They were speechless. Finally, Jimmy grinned sheepishly at Nick and asked, "I wonder what he did with our fish?"

GHOSTS OF THE

MATANZAS

*I*n the summer of 1565 the French and Spanish were playing a cat-and-mouse game of conquest to see who could win the North American continent. The French Protestant, Jean Ribault, had established Fort Caroline in the vicinity of Jacksonville. As the French presence grew, King Philip II of Spain commissioned Admiral Pedro Menéndez de Avilés to oust the French and settle Florida for Spain.

Menéndez arrived at St. Augustine, claimed the land for His Most Catholic Majesty, and immediately began off-loading supplies for the new outpost. Ribault was only hours behind, and Menéndez knew from his long experience at sea that a hurricane was brewing. Realizing that Ribault would not arrive for days because of the hurricane, Menéndez marched north to capture Fort Caroline.

As he correctly surmised, the French fleet was all but demolished, and a week later Native Americans informed him that three of Ribault's ships had been wrecked near Ponce de Leon Inlet and that one hundred remaining survivors had marched north to Anastasia Island. Menéndez marched south with a company of soldiers to meet the Frenchman. Having neither guards nor food for a hundred prisoners, he slaughtered them, and the waters of the inlet ran red with French blood. The bay, the river, and the inlet became known as the Matanzas, meaning "the slaughters."

The "Ghosts of the Matanzas" ghost tour is a unique cruise of Matanzas Bay aboard the magnificent seventy-two-foot schooner *Freedom*. It combines history, fantasy, legend, ghosts, and a lot of fun in the dark haunted waters off St. Augustine, and the tour guide, in the form of pirate Captain Andrew Wiggins, relates the story of the slaughter of the Huguenots and many other tales in passionate detail.

Wiggins claims to have been the quartermaster for the privateer Robert Searles. In 1667 when France and Spain declared war on each other, a French surgeon, Pierre Piquet, quietly took passage on a supply ship leaving St. Augustine. Searles seized the ship off the coast of Cuba. Dr. Piquet had some interesting information for Captain Searles. The Spanish had salvaged a treasure ship off the coast, and its cargo of silver ingots was in the royal treasury in St. Augustine.

Searles and his crew sailed the captured ship back into St. Augustine disguised as Spaniards. In the middle of the night, the privateers went ashore to seize the silver and whatever else they could lay their hands on. The small Spanish garrison under Sergeant Major Ponce de Leon II fled into the woods. During the raid, Searles and his men also killed sixty civilians in the streets, including the sergeant major's young daughter. Legend has it that Searles shot five-year-old Faviana himself.

After the attack Searles lay in his bed with a bottle of rum and his blood lust gradually waned. It was then that the image of this little girl came to haunt him. Of all the people murdered that night, only the spirit of Faviana was courageous enough to rise from the dead and torment Searles. Her ghost bedeviled him night after night until he could take no more, and he weighed anchor. Still, the ghost of Faviana hounded him, until he finally took his own life with his pistol. That is the legend. We do know that Robert Searles dropped out of history after this raid, never to be mentioned again.

Captain Wiggins tells other fascinating stories of the lady pirates, Ann Bonnie and Mary Reed, and Captain Calico Jack. He also recounts the ghostly legends of local fisherman who see strange sights and hear strange sounds on the bay at night.

Captain Wiggins spins these tales with breathless speed and intersperses them with games, songs, and magic tricks. The one-hour cruise with so many stories oriented seaward provides a completely different perspective of St. Augustine. And floating silently on the black waters of Matanzas Bay, his stories are captivating—and scary. The "Ghosts of the Matanzas" ghost tour is a memorable experience.

Interestingly, my sensitive friend, Jennifer Pastore, called me several months ago with a fascinating theory. After driving around Anastasia Island for some time, she came to the conclusion that the French Huguenots were not murdered at the inlet or on the landward side of the island but had been marched across the dunes to the beach, out of sight of the town. We drove to the area that she thought might have been the location of the massacre. The site is very near to the house in the "Gateway to Hell" story in *Ghosts of St. Augustine*. Could the oppressive ghostly activity in that house be connected to the tormented lost Huguenot souls who were slaughtered near there so long ago?

SIGHTINGS

*T*he Mill Top at the north end of St. George Street is one of my favorite spots in St. Augustine. Sitting outside on one of the open-air decks shaded by the giant live-oak tree, I'm in a tree house, high above the town with a splendid view of the Castillo and the bay. In the summer, even on the hottest days, a gentle breeze always seems to be blowing. And in the winter cold with the heavy clear plastic curtains drawn and the heaters blasting, the tavern is a warm and cozy place to watch the world go by. The Mill Top is a popular gathering spot for locals and tourists alike.

No one knows for sure what was on the site during the hundreds of years of St. Augustine's existence, probably a series of houses. And, being so close to the Castillo and to the north gates, the area must have experienced innumerable disasters. The many hurricanes that have swept along the coast of north Florida most certainly destroyed whatever was built on the site, flooding the occupants out on more than one occasion. And the location had to have known the torch from James Moore's raid in 1702 and General James Oglethorpe's aborted invasion in 1740.

What is documented is that Walter B. Fraser built a gristmill on the site in the 1930s. The overshot wheel was powered by an artesian well, and the mill itself was on the second story. The mill was rebuilt in 1947, and in 1996 W. Angyalfy and J. R. Fraser reconstructed it again. Although the water-powered wheel still runs, the mill has been removed from the second floor, which is now the Mill Top Tavern.

With its stressed, pock-marked wood and open beams, the place looks haunted—and it is. Its creaky old bones fairly moan, especially late at night when all is quiet. One morning at 2:30, just after closing, Kevin and Penny, the bartenders working that night, were sitting at a table in the bar area counting the receipts for the night. They had locked all the windows and doors, including the French doors, which opened out onto the covered deck. It was windy outside, and the building really was moaning. The two heard a noise at the French doors and both looked up just in time to see the specials menu board, which had been sitting on top of the cigarette machine by the ladies restroom, fly straight across the room and crash into a framed poster on the far wall, shattering both the menu board and the glass covering the poster. Kevin and Penny were stunned and petrified. After some minutes, they looked at each other and without a word, threw the money in the bag, locked up, and rushed out of the place.

Says Kevin, "That's one of the reasons I don't like working late. I've been here a couple of times just by myself after everyone else has left, and it's not a good feeling. It's like someone is watching me."

Kelly, another bartender, doesn't have a problem. "Oh, yeah, there have been lots of times when I've been up here late by myself. I've been sitting here counting money, and the locked windows will open and close. In fact, the first time it happened, I went over to one of the windows after it had just gone up and then down, thinking that maybe I was just seeing something. The window was locked, so I thought I was definitely seeing things. So when it went up again, I raced over. Sure enough, the window was opened. I backed away from it, and it went down. Then I stepped forward to look, and you guessed it. The window was locked. Lots of times things get moved, you know, glasses, a clipboard, just stuff. Doesn't bother me, though. Except for the incident with Kevin and Penny, whoever and whatever does this is harmless and nonviolent."

On another occasion Will and some friends were sitting inside listening to Don, an institution at the Mill Top, play and sing some of his soulful songs. Will's friend took a picture of Don while he was performing. Several days later Will came back up in the middle of the day with a picture, the photograph of Don his friend had made. There, reflected in the window to the right of the bandstand, was the image of a woman wearing a long, Victorian-style dress and hat. No one has yet figured out where the image came from.

*   *   *   *

Carol Ann's mother moved in with her a year ago last September. She was getting older and couldn't live by herself anymore. Carol Ann had just purchased a big triple-wide trailer on the outskirts of St. Augustine, but she and her mother shared her single-wide waiting for the big one to be delivered.

Her mother became ill just before Thanksgiving and she was in the hospital for so long she never got to see the new house until

Mother's Day weekend, when Carol Ann brought her home. The end was near for her mother and Carol Ann wanted her to die at home in her own bed. On June 23 her mother had a major stroke and passed away, having lived barely a month in the new house. Her death was very peaceful. Carol Ann, her daughters, and grandchildren were with her when she died.

Carol Ann's daughter had given her a floor lamp that was "older than I am." It had two bulbs, each on a separate pull chain switch. Four days after her mother died, Carol Ann got up in the morning to go to work and found the light on, both bulbs. She did not remember turning it on the night before. In fact, she thought it was strange, because she wouldn't normally have done that. She turned one side off, but the other side was frozen solid. The chain just wouldn't pull. So, she unscrewed the bulb part way and went on to work.

She came home later and after eating and watching a little TV, turned off all the lights, and went to bed. The next morning when she arose, the light was back on. Again, exasperated, she turned one side off and tried to pull the chain on the frozen side. It still wouldn't pull, so she started unscrewing the bulb even more than the day before. Then, she suddenly realized. "Okay, all right, Mom. I got it. You're talking to me. Everything is fine. I needed to hear that. I love you."

That afternoon when Carol Ann returned home from work, she found a flashlight that had been missing for two weeks in the middle of the living room floor in front of the TV. The only thing she had used it for was to walk the dog when it was dark out. She knew she had just misplaced it, but for it to show up in the middle of the living room? That was weird. She knew the dog hadn't found it and placed it in front of the TV. He wasn't that smart. Well, she was busy and left the flashlight lying there while she ran around getting things done. A few minutes later she came back through the living room, and the flashlight was still lying there—but now it was turned on. "Okay, Mom. You can go on. I miss you."

And that's the last contact Carol Ann had with her mother.

*   *   *   *

"I used to work in the old house in the Spanish Quarter as an interpreter and one day I was giving a tour to about ten or twelve people," relates Annie. "Now I was told in this house in the upstairs child's bedroom room never to open the shutters. In those old Spanish homes they have the window and then the shutter on the inside. Well, I thought this was ridiculous. The room was dark; we didn't have electricity in the house, so I opened the shutter. And the room was all nice and sunny. It looked great. Well, I have my tour group come in, and I'm explaining to them about the bed and all the things in the room. And all of a sudden it was like this gray cloud just swished through the room and the shutters banged closed violently. Everybody asked, 'What was that?' I said, 'I think we just saw a ghost!' I never opened the shutters again."

*   *   *   *

Rebecca Barksdale's mother and grandmother are both very sensitive, but Rebecca had never had any experiences herself—until last March. She and her family had visited St. Augustine often since she was a girl of twelve. In March she and her husband came for a visit, and the sensitivity issue was in the back of her mind. The first night they were there, they went on the A Ghostly Experience Walking Tour. The tour was very interesting, but Rebecca was disappointed—nothing happened, although she did take some pictures that proved interesting later.

The second night they went on the Haunted Lighthouse Tour. As they were beginning the tour a small cat appeared, and, being an animal lover, Rebecca picked it up and played with it. As the tour guide began telling the history of the lighthouse, she felt a cold chill descend around her, the coldest she'd ever felt, bone chilling, spine tingling, hair standing on end, goose bumps. At the same time, the little cat hissed, jumped out of her arms and disappeared.

As the tour progressed into the park where the ghosts of two little girls are often seen, she began to feel as if someone was behind her. She turned to look. No one was there. And as they passed through the park, her eyes were constantly drawn to the swings, although they hung motionless, and she did hear giggling and footsteps.

The tour continued around the grounds and they came to a stop by the keeper's house. Rebecca looked through the window and suddenly caught a glimpse of what looked like a body hanging. Moments later, the tour guide told them the story of the man who hanged himself in the house and of his ghost, which is still seen hanging from the rafters. Rebecca was scared and elated at the same time.

The next day they went back to the lighthouse for the regular tour and climbed to the top. She is terrified of heights, but forced herself to climb anyway. All the way up she could hear footsteps behind her and could smell roses. There are no roses on the grounds of the lighthouse. At the top she smelled cigar smoke, and, of course, there is no smoking in the lighthouse. She smelled the cigar all the way down and, oddly enough, wasn't frightened at all. Was the ghost of the lightkeeper who fell to his death so long ago helping her down the steps?

The last night of their stay, Rebecca and her husband were strolling around the Castillo, when she heard a beautiful female voice singing and the name Christina came into her mind. And she also sensed that Christina's own people accidentally killed her on the grounds of the Castillo. Rebecca was never able to verify any of that, but knew in her heart it was true.

Rebecca hasn't had any experiences at home, but she's waiting with great anticipation for her husband to take her back to St. Augustine so she can explore her newfound gifts.

*   *   *   *

Last year was not a good year for Sandy. She was caring for her father, who had Alzheimer's. At one point in the spring, she rented the movie *Michael*, in which John Travolta is an angel. Her father and the whole family enjoyed it very much. A couple of weeks later she happened to go upstairs in her house, and when she came down she saw a small, white feather on the stairs. She thought that was a bit odd, because she hadn't seen it going up. But she was preoccupied thinking about her father.

However, a month later Sandy was talking to her close friend, Elaine, about her father, and another small, white feather floated down from nowhere and landed on her hand. Now she suspected something. An angelic message?

In early summer she and her family went to vacation at their cabin in North Carolina. In preparation she packed her father's and mother's medications in a cloth bag. When they arrived at the cabin, Sandy began unpacking, and when she emptied the cloth bag, she found a third small, white feather. She was astounded.

Finally, in the middle of July she and her husband, Jim, were sitting at the picnic table in their backyard discussing what they would do with her father, who was getting increasingly worse. Sandy was very worried about him and hated to see him wasting away. While they were talking, she happened to look beyond Jim and saw, yes, a small, white feather floating slowly to the earth. But just before it landed a gust of wind picked it up and carried it into the sky and out of sight. Sandy knew then that God was calling her father home. He passed away five days later.

*   *   *   *

Angela has a boyfriend—a spirit boyfriend. He seems to like her a lot, because he's always hanging around. She calls him Chris, and she has become very comfortable with him. Once when a group of kids where over, Angela's sister saw Chris walking down the hall towards her room. Her sister slept with Angela that night. On another occasion a girlfriend was spending the night and sleeping on the floor in Angela's room. In the middle of the night, she woke Angela up and asked her to stop snoring. Angela laughed, "It's not me. It's Chris."

"Who's Chris?" her friend asked. Then she looked up and saw someone lying on the bed next to Angela. She screamed, pulled the covers over her head, and pretended to go back to sleep, although she didn't sleep a wink the rest of the night.

Angela likes having Chris around. She doesn't see him that often, but all her friends know about him. And what date is going to get fresh when a ghost is looking over his shoulder?

*   *   *   *

A family of four, father, mother, and two young boys about six and eight, was spending the weekend at The Painted Lady. One evening they all went on the A Ghostly Experience Walking Tour and went to the fort to hear the ghost stories. The tour group was large and a little strung out. The mother was with the six-year-old at one end and the father with the eight-year-old at the other.

After the tour they headed back up Avenida de Menendez to the B&B. While they were walking the mother said to her husband, "Wait until you hear what Jimmy saw on the parapet of the fort." Jimmy explained that he'd seen a glowing, greenish specter with a tricorn hat and a old military uniform.

The father and Jimmy's brother stopped abruptly. "I don't believe it. Bryan just told me he'd seen the same thing."

Both boys from two different locations had seen an eighteenth-century Spanish artilleryman standing next to a cannon on the parapet of the Castillo.

IN CLOSING

I began collecting ghost stories in St. Augustine ten years ago. At first I saw them only as oral history. But the more I talked to people and the more research I did, I came to realize that these paranormal events are occurring today and with increasing regularity. In fact, I think most people have had an experience that they cannot explain. I do know that those who are sensitive enough to be aware of spirits are having more and more encounters in St. Augustine.

Over the past several years much paranormal research has been done in St. Augustine to try and understand the reason for this increase in activity, and yet no one can explain it. As for me, I'm just satisfied with a good story.

In spite of my wanderings in the Ancient City, I have not yet seen a ghost, but I have had some spine-tingling experiences. My after-hours visits to both the Old Jail and to Ripley's had my skin crawling when I left. And at the Kenwood Inn I met both Lavender and Raymond—I think.

Kerrianne and I were standing in the lobby of the inn and talking about smells involving ghosts. She said that she seldom smelled anything when she experienced the presence of spirits in the inn, but suddenly I was enveloped by the odor of a sweet perfume. I said, "I can't smell much myself, except I do detect your perfume right now." She smiled, "I'm not wearing perfume. I guess Lavender is trying to cross me up."

A few minutes later, I took some pictures and we stood talking with some of Kerrianne's guests about Raymond and his chair. I was holding my camera when it abruptly turned itself off. It doesn't turn off automatically, and I hadn't had my finger anywhere near the on-off button. I hadn't even moved my hand. It just turned itself off— or was it Raymond?

And, of course, I had that experience with the wobbly tape at the Antique Mall. So, I guess I can say I've had some ghostly experiences. In any case, I am going to continue my quest for a face-to-face encounter with a spirit, and I hope he or she is as kind and gentle as the rest of the ghosts of St. Augustine.

Author Dave Lapham, a retired Marine officer, lives with his wife in Orlando, Florida, where he has continued his writing career with this second collection of ghost stories from his favorite city, St. Augustine. He is currently working on a novel, and, yes, it will have ghosts.

Artist Tom Lapham is Dave's older brother and also a retired Marine officer. Tom lives in Springfield, Virginia, with his wife and two poodles, Rosie and Edgar Allan Poo, and his work can be seen in the Commerce Street Gallery in Occoquan, Virginia.

If you enjoyed reading this book, here are some other books from Pineapple Press on related topics. For a complete catalog, write to Pineapple Press, P.O. Box 3889, Sarasota, FL 34230 or call 1-800-PINEAPL (746-3275). Or visit our website at www.pineapplepress.com.

Ghosts of St. Augustine by Dave Lapham. The unique and often turbulent history of America's oldest city is told in twenty-four spooky stories that cover four hundred years' worth of ghosts. ISBN 1-56164-123-5 (pb)

Oldest Ghosts by Karen Harvey. In St. Augustine (the oldest settlement in the New World), the ghost apparitions are as intriguing as the city's history. ISBN 1-56164-222-3 (pb)

Houses of St. Augustine by David Nolan. A history of the city told through its buildings, from the earliest coquina structures, through the colonial and Victorian times, to the modern era. Color photographs and original watercolors. ISBN 1-56164-069-7 (hb), ISBN 1-56164-075-1 (pb)

Haunt Hunter's Guide to Florida by Joyce Elson Moore. Discover the general history and "haunt" history of numerous sites around the state where ghosts reside. ISBN 1-56164-150-2 (pb)

Haunted Lighthouses and How to Find Them by George Steitz. The producer of the popular TV series *Haunted Lighthouses* takes you on a tour of America's most enchanting and mysterious lighthouses. ISBN 1-56164-268-1 (pb)

Haunting Sunshine by Jack Powell. Take a wild ride though the shadows of the Sunshine State in this collection of deliciously creepy stories of ghosts in the theatres, churches, and historic places of Florida. ISBN 1-56164-220-7 (pb)

Ghosts of the Carolina Coasts by Terrance Zepke. Taken from real-life occurrences and Carolina Lowcountry lore, these thirty-two spine-tingling ghost stories take place in prominent historic structures of the region. ISBN 1-56164-175-8 (pb)

Best Ghost Tales of North Carolina and *Best Ghost Tales of South Carolina*. The actors of Carolina's past linger among the living in these thrilling collection of ghost tales. Experience the chilling encounters told by the winners of the North Carolina "Ghost Watch" contest. Use Zepke's tips to conduct your own ghost hunt. ISBN 1-56164-233-9 (pb); 1-56164-306-8 (pb)